EVERYONE WANTS A SAVIOR,

FEW WANT A LORD

The Author

WESTBOW
PRESS®
A DIVISION OF THOMAS NELSON
& ZONDERVAN

Scripture taken from the King James Version of the Bible.

Scripture quotations marked (TLB) are taken from The Living Bible copyright © 1971. Used by permission of Tyndale House Publishers, Inc., Carol Stream, Illinois 60188. All rights reserved.

WestBow Press books may be ordered through booksellers or by contacting:

WestBow Press
A Division of Thomas Nelson & Zondervan
1663 Liberty Drive
Bloomington, IN 47403
www.westbowpress.com
1 (866) 928-1240

ISBN: 978-1-9736-1665-8 (sc)
ISBN: 978-1-9736-1667-2 (hc)
ISBN: 978-1-9736-1666-5 (e)

Library of Congress Control Number: 2018901021

Print information available on the last page.

WestBow Press rev. date: 3/15/2018

CONTENTS

ACKNOWLEDGEMENTS

There is only one to acknowledge for this book and that is
The King of kings and Lord of lords
It is His Spirit who will determine the Spiritual growth success
of those who read what He has had me write on these pages.

Through the years (and they are many) God has spoken to me through many great Christians, such as Mark Arant, David Jeremiah, Max Lucado, Joyce Meyer, Dean Overton, Adrian Rogers, Harold Salem, Michael Youseff and others too numerous to remember. I thank God for these great people. Whom God spoke through to these great Christians, I do not know. My prayer is that God will speak to you through this book, thereby continuing God's message.

My wonderful Christian wife, who is my greatest earthly God-given gift, has been patient, loving, and inspirational to me. I love her and thank her.

Lastly, in a small Midwestern state, in a small town (pop. 800 which may include a few dogs and cats), in a small (average attendance 25-30) church, in that small church's basement corner is a small Sunday school group (average 6-7) of faithful Christians who because of their faithfulness enhanced this book and encouraged their Sunday school teacher to allow God to speak through him. Because we asked in faith, God had perfect attendance. And, if God can find us in that little church basement corner, He can find you.

Because I want God to receive all the glory this book will bring, I have borrowed "Smokey The Bear's" middle name for my first pen name, "The." When you think about it, "The" may catch on as a great first name, The Anderson, The Barton, The Erickson, The Hughes, The Russell, The Shoen. Kind of catchy isn't it!

My surname, "Author", needs some explaining. I am not the Author of every good and perfect gift (James 1:17), but He is my Father. (John 1:12)

James 1:17 *Every good and every perfect gift is from above and cometh down from the Father of lights, with whom is no variableness, neither shadow of turning.*

John 1:12 *But as many as received Him, to them gave He power to become the sons of God, even to them that believe on His name.*

P.S. If this is your book, I encourage you to highlight or mark the words or phrases that are meaningful to you.

FOREWORD

This book is not for leisurely reading, but for thoughtful contemplation.

Jesus spoke in parables and gave words of wisdom. This book's objective through God-inspiring parables and words of wisdom is for you to hear God's loving, heavenly offer to dine in paradise with Him and avoid the screams and wailings in the Lake of Fire.

Jesus, who stands at the door of our souls and knocks (Revelation 3:20), could blow that door and the wall it's hinged on off the face of the universe, but He doesn't. You must open the door. You must invite Him in. When you earnestly do, your joy will know no bounds. God's true Spirit will change your life by enhancing your peace, lightening (not eliminating) your burdens, and filling the void in you with His Spirit.

Revelation 3:20, Behold, I stand at the door and knock; if any man hears My voice and opens the door, I will come in to him, and will sup with him, and he with Me.

So, let's give it a try!

First step, **Pray that God will speak to you through these pages and what He says will never leave your heart**. If you really want to know if there is a God; if you really want to know if He loves you;

if you really want to know how He can speak to you; if you really want to know what the God who created you has for you; then pray the above prayer. He <u>may</u> speak to you anyway, but if you pray this prayer sincerely, He <u>will</u> make Himself known to you.

<u>John 7:17</u> *If any man will do His will, he shall know of the doctrine, whether it be of God or whether it is merely My own.*

<u>Matthew 7:9</u> *Or what man is there of you whom if his son ask for bread will give him a stone?*

It's exciting!

I have already prayed for you. I'm eager for us someday to dine together in paradise with the one true loving God.

The Author

The surgeon's main duty is not to come into the operating room, hold the patient's hand, and tell him he is healthy. Rather, the surgeon comes committed with a knife (Matthew 10:34) and the skills to make the patient better. After surgery, the patient's main duty is to follow the medical advice given to progressively improve in health (Matthew 12:43-45). The patient's future well-being lies in his commitment (John 8:10–11), not in the surgeon's commitment.

Matthew 10:34 Think not that I have come to send peace. I came not to send peace but a sword.

Matthew 12:43-45 When the unclean spirit is gone out of the man, he walks through dry places, seeking rest and finds none. Then he says, "I will return into my house from which I came out."; and when he is come, he finds it empty, swept, and garnished. Then he goes and takes with himself seven other spirits more wicked than himself, and they enter in and dwell there: and the last state of that man is worse than the first.

Don't pick up a heavy load the wrong way.

Matthew 11:29–30 Take My yoke upon you, and learn of Me; for I am meek and lowly of heart and you shall find rest for your souls; for My yoke is easy, and My burden is light.

Christians may be nuts, but they're attached to a great bolt.

John 10:3–4 The gatekeeper opens the gate for him and the sheep hear his voice and come to him; and he calls his own by name and leads them out. He walks ahead of them, and they follow him for they recognize his voice.

Just like insurance companies, all religions are perfectly good until you need them.

<u>Matthew 24:24–27 TLB</u> For false Christs shall arise and false prophets, and will do wonderful miracles so that if it were possible even God's chosen ones would be deceived. See, I have warned you. So, if someone tells you the Messiah has returned and is out in the desert, don't bother to go and look. Or, that He is hiding in a certain place, don't believe it. For as the lightning flashes across the sky from east to west, so shall My coming be, When I, the Son of all mankind, return.

<u>John 14:6</u> Jesus said unto him, I am the way, the truth, and the life; no man cometh unto the Father, but by Me.

<u>1 John 5:20–21 TLB</u> And we know that Christ, God's Son, has come to help us understand and find the true God. And now we are in God because we are in Jesus Christ, His Son, who is the only true God; and He is eternal life. Dear children keep away from anything that might take God's place in your hearts. Amen.

Quoting scripture will not get you to heaven (Matthew 4:6); doing miracles will not (Matthew 7: 22-23), neither will believing there <u>is a</u> God (James 2:19). But, faith (Romans 14:23) <u>in</u> the one true God (I John 5:20) by doing His will (John 14:23) assures you of the kingdom of heaven.

<u>Matthew 4:6</u> And the devil said unto Jesus, "If thou be the Son of God, cast thyself down: for it is written, He shall give His angels charge over Thee, and in their hands they shall bear Thee up, lest at any time Thou dash Thy foot against a stone.

Matthew 7:22-23 Many shall say unto Me in that day, Lord, Lord, have we not prophesied in Thy name? And in Thy name have we not cast out devils; and in Thy name done many wonderful works? And then will I profess unto them, "I never knew you. Depart from Me you that do iniquity."

James 2:19 You believe that there is one God; you do well; the devils also believe and tremble.

Romans 14:23 TLB Anyone who believes that something he wants to do is wrong shouldn't do it. He sins if he does, for he thinks it is wrong, and so for him, it is wrong. For whatsoever is not of faith is wrong.

1 John 5:20 TLB We know Christ, God's Son, has come to help us understand and find the true God. And now we are in God because we are in Christ Jesus, His Son, who is the only true God; and He is eternal life.

John 14:23 Jesus answered unto him and said, "If a man love me, he will keep My words: and My Father will love him, and we will come unto him and live with him.

After graduating from college and still not finding Mr. Right, Barbie, the designated bridesmaid, watched as her friends married. This beautiful Christian woman prayed, "Lord, please help me find my future husband. Lord, why don't you help?" Weeks turned into months, and many prayers were pleaded before Barbie met her "Mr. Right."

Reflecting, Barbie realized that although she was ready for marriage, Mr. Right was not. Mr. Right had to leave the country, meet Christian missionaries who introduced him to Jesus, and begin to grow spiritually. When he was ready to be a proper Christian husband and father, God introduced Barbie to him. It wasn't Barbie who wasn't ready for marriage; it was her future husband whom God was preparing. When everything is right, God will act. Don't confuse God's delays with God's denials.

__Ecclesiastes 3:1,4__ To everything there is a season, and a time to every purpose under the heaven; a time to weep, a time to laugh; a time to mourn, and a time to dance.

__Romans 12:2__ Be not conformed to this world: but be ye transformed by the renewing of your mind that ye may prove what is that good, and acceptable, and perfect will of God.

Barbie's patience allowed God to do His perfect will.

__Romans 8:25__ But if we must keep trusting God for something that hasn't happened yet, it teaches us to wait patiently and confidently.

The truth is very narrow-minded. You cannot compromise, tweak, rewrite, deny, or alter the truth and still have truth. Believing there is no God does not eliminate God; describing God to fit your desires does not change God.

__John 14:6__ Jesus said unto him, I am the way, the truth, and the life; no man cometh unto the Father, but by Me.

__Isaiah 45:22 TLB__ Let all the world look to Me for salvation! For I am God; there is no other.

During "Career Day," a 16-year old 8th-grade dropout told a graduate student working on her Masters in Business Administration degree to quit school. The dropout stated that when he did, his life was more fun with less homework and more free time.

On opening day of major league baseball, a young man in the stands shouted at the American League's Most Valuable Player to quit baseball. When he was in Little League, he quit and had more fun with video games, less pressure, and no practices.

While jogging through the park, a fitness-trainer hears someone yelling, "Stop!" The obese, breathless man waddles to the jogger with this advice, "Stop exercising," he gasps. When I quit exercising my life got easier, no more exhausting, tiring exercises, more time for eating the foods I like, videos, and friends, etc. (Hebrews 5:12)

On my way to a prayer meeting I have regularly attended for years, I stopped at a convenience store to fill my car with gas. The person across from me filling her car started a conversation and found where I was headed. She gave me this advice. Save your breath and time. I prayed once and nothing happened.

Would the graduate student tell the dropout to quit school? Would the American League's Most Valuable Player tell a Little Leaguer it wasn't worth it? Would a fitness trainer tell an obese person to quit exercising? Quitting is easy without a desire to reach a worthy goal. The "*go*" in "*goal*" is the key. *No "go" no "goal"* When someone encourages you to quit, ask what maturity level he reached in his goal's journey.

Jesus never said it would be easy (John 15:20). He said it would be worth it (Revelation 21:4, Romans 8:18).

Hebrews 5:12 For whatever God says to us is full of living power and is sharper than the sharpest dagger, cutting swift and deep into our innermost thoughts and desires with all their parts, and is a discerner of the thoughts and intents of the heart.

John 15:20 Remember the word I said unto you, "The servant is not greater than his lord. If they have persecuted Me, they will also persecute you; if they have kept My saying, they will keep yours also."

Revelation 21:4 And God shall wipe away all tears from their eyes; and there shall be no more death, neither sorrow, nor crying, neither shall there be any more pain: for the former things are passed away.

Romans 8:18 For I reckon that the sufferings of this present time are not worthy to be compared with the glory which shall be revealed to us.

The Maker of the stars (Genesis 1:16) would rather die for you than live without you. (Romans 5:8)

Genesis 1:16 And God made two great lights; the greater light to rule the day, and the lesser to rule the night; he made the stars also.

Romans 5:8 But commanded his love toward us in that while we were yet sinners, Christ died for us.

The Holy Spirit (God's Spirit) points out flaws to cleanse us. (John 14:26, 1 John 1:9) Satan points out flaws to condemn us. (2 Corinthians 7:10, Matthew 26:74, Matthew 27:3–5) Both Peter and Judas sinned. When choosing, know the difference between cleansing and condemning (1 Peter 5:8). Satan is *NOT* a spokesperson for God (Genesis 3:4–5). If Judas had sought cleansing from Jesus and asked for forgiveness, he would have found it (Matthew 7:7). Instead, he succumbed to Satan's destructive desire.

__John 14:26__ But the Comforter which is the Holy Spirit whom the father will send in my name, He shall teach you all things, and bring all things to your remembrance, whatsoever I have said unto you.

__1 John 1:9__ If we confess our sins, He is faithful and just to forgive us our sins, and to cleanse us from all unrighteousness.

__2 Corinthians 7:10 TLB__ For God sometimes uses sorrow in our lives to help us turn away from sin and seek eternal life. We should never regret His sending it. But the sorrow of the man who is not a Christian is not the sorrow of true repentance and does not prevent eternal death.

__Matthew 26:74 TLB__ Peter began to curse and swear, "I don't even know the man." And immediately the cock crowed.

__Matthew 27:3-5__ About that time Judas who had betrayed Jesus, when he saw that Jesus had been condemned to die, changed his mind and deeply regretted what he had done and brought back the money to the chief priests and other Jewish leaders. "I have sinned," he declared, "for I have betrayed an innocent man." "That's your problem," they retorted. Then he threw the money onto the floor of the temple floor and went out and hanged himself.

__1 Peter 5:8__ Be sober, be vigilant, because your adversary the devil, as a roaring lion, walks about seeking whom he may devour.

Genesis 3:4–5 And the serpent said unto the woman, Ye shall not surely die for God doth know that in the day ye eat thereof, then your eyes shall be opened, and ye shall be as gods knowing good and evil.

Matthew 7:7 Ask and it will be given you, seek and ye shall find, knock and it shall be opened unto you.

When Satan reminds you of your past, remind him of his future (Romans 6:6–8, Revelation 20:10). It is not what you are separated from (sin, death) that counts, but what you are separated to (Jesus). (2 Corinthians 5:17)

Romans 6:6–8 TLB Your old evil desires were nailed to the cross with Him; that part of you that loves to sin was crushed and fatally wounded, so that your sin-loving body is no longer under sin's control, no longer needs to be a slave to sin; for when you are deadened to sin you are freed from all its allure and it's power over you. And since your old sin-loving nature "died" with Christ, we know that you will share His new life.

Revelation 20:10 And the devil that deceived them was cast into the lake of fire and brimstone, where the beast and the false prophet are and shall be tormented day and night forever and ever.

2 Corinthians 5:17 Therefore, if any man be of Christ, he is a new creature: old things are passed away; behold, all things are become new.

There are no losers with Jesus, only winners and learners.

Matthew 11:28-30 Come unto me all you that are labor and are heavy laden, and I will give you rest. Take my yoke upon you, and learn from me; for I am meek and lowly in heart; and ye shall find rest unto your souls; for my yoke is easy, and my burden is light.

Satan doesn't always fight churches, he often joins them.

1Thessalonians 3:5 For this cause, when I could no longer forbear, I sent to know your faith, lest the tempter have tempted you, and our labor be in vain.

John 13:21,27 TLB (at the last Supper meal) Now Jesus was in great anguish of spirit and exclaimed, "Yes, it is true – one of you will betray Me." As soon as Judas had eaten it, Satan entered into him. Then Jesus told him, "Hurry-do it now."

Ignorance is not bliss.

1 Thessalonians 4:13 But, I would not have you to be ignorant, brethren, concerning them which are asleep, that ye sorrow not, even as others which have no hope.

Christians should *not* be fearful of Christ's second coming or death. It will be like the end of the NCAA Championship game when the final horn sounds. As winners we will be cheering excitedly, running, jumping, and hugging each other. We were built for this moment!

The losers, on the other hand, will be regretfully hanging their heads, crying, and shockingly stunned. During the tournament many teams are believed to be the champion, but after the final buzzer is sounded, everyone knows the winner. (Philippians 2:10-11)

We, the winners, will joyfully run toward the official who is holding the trophy and not be fearful. The game is over; the trophy won; the goal reached.

In that victorious moment when we are on our way to the heavenly victory party, and we turn to a teammate to shout, "We won," we won't even think of all the trials and heart breaks life gave us. The pain it took is overwhelmingly outmatched by the victorious joy we are experiencing (Luke 6:23, 1 Peter 4:13). Immediately, we will recognize Jesus as the loving Savior whom He said He was as He takes us to heaven's victory party. (1 Thessalonians 4: 16-17)

Philippians 2:10-11 *That at the name of Jesus every knee shall bow in heaven and on earth, and under the earth, and every tongue shall confess that Jesus Christ is Lord, to the glory of God the Father.*

Luke 6:23 *Rejoice in that day and leap for joy; for behold your reward is great in heaven; for in like manner did their fathers unto the prophets.*

1 Peter 4:13 *Rejoice, inasmuch as you are partakers of Christ's suffering; that, when His glory is revealed, you may be glad also with exceeding joy.*

1 Thessalonians 4:16-17 *For the Lord himself shall descend from heaven with a shout, with the voice of the archangel, and with the trump of God; and the dead in Christ shall rise first. Then we which are alive and remain shall be caught up together with them in the clouds to meet the Lord in the air and so shall we ever be with the Lord.*

Jesus never said it would be easy (John 16:33). He said it would be worth it (Revelation 21:4, 7, 2:26).

Romans 8:18 *For I reckon that the sufferings of this present time are not worthy to be compared with the glory which shall be revealed in us.*

Revelation 21:4,7 TLB *He will wipe away all tears from their eyes, and there shall be no more death, or sorrow, or crying, or pain. All of that has gone forever. Everyone who conquers will inherit all these blessings, and I will be his God and he will be my son.*

Revelation 2:26 *And he that overcomes, and keeps my works unto the end, to him will I give power over the nations.*

When looking for God's "word," you must "knock the 'L'" out of this "world!"

Romans 12:21 *Be not overcome by evil, but overcome evil with good.*

2 Peter 2:19 TLB *"You aren't saved by being good," they say, 'so you might as well be bad. Do what you like, be free." But these very teachers who offer you this "freedom" from the law are themselves slaves to sin and destruction. For a man is a slave to whatever controls him.*

Satan does more harm by sowing weeds than by pulling wheat.

Matthew 23:13 TLB *Woe to you Pharisees, and you other religious leaders, Hypocrites! For you won't let others enter the Kingdom of heaven, and won't go in yourselves. And you pretend to be holy, with all your long public prayers in the streets, while you are evicting widows from their homes. Hypocrites!*

Matthew 13:29-30 *But he said, "Nay," lest while you gather up the weeds, you root up also the wheat with them. Let both grow together until the harvest, and in the time of harvest I will say unto the reapers. Gather first the weeds, and bind them in bundles to burn. But, gather the wheat into my barn."*

There are no overachievers with God. "Overachieving" is a subjective term. Our prisons are full of overachievers.

Philippians 4:13 *I can do all things through Christ who strengthens me.*

John 15:5 *I am the vine you are the branches. He that abides in me and I in him, the same brings forth much fruit: for without me you can do nothing.*

Either you are a missionary or a mission field.

Luke 11: 23 *He that is not with Me is against Me, and he that gathers not with Me scatters.*

Sadly, many people, like peacocks, strut to Hell looking too good to be damned.

Matthew 19:30 *But many that are first shall be last; and the last shall be first.*

Luke 16:15 *And He said to them, "You are they which justify yourselves before man; but God knows your hearts: for that which is highly esteemed among men is abomination in the sight of God."*

Luke 20:46-47 *Beware of the scribes which desire to walk in long robes, and love greetings in the markets, and the higher seats in the synagogues, and the chief rooms at feasts. But even while they are praying long prayers with great outward piety, they are planning schemes to cheat widows out of their property. Therefore, God's heaviest sentenced awaits these men.*

Reading the Bible will save you as quickly as reading a prescription will heal you.

<u>Acts 8:28-31</u> And now an Ethiopian eunuch was returning in his chariot, reading aloud from the book of the prophet, Isaiah. The Holy Spirit said to Philip, "Go over and walk along beside the chariot. Philip ran over and heard what he was reading and asked, "Do you understand it?" "Of course not!" the man replied. "How can I when there is no one to instruct me?" And he begged Philip to come up into the chariot and sit with him.

Rather than pray and study the scriptures for God's guidance, a less passionate Christian closed his eyes, randomly opened the Bible and pointed to a verse from the randomly picked page for God's guidance. One day as he was using this method, he opened to Matthew 27:5. He quickly closed the Bible and reopened it to Luke 10:37!

<u>Liv Matthew 27:5</u> Then Judas threw the money onto the floor of the Temple and went out and hanged himself.

<u>Luke 10:37</u> ... Then said Jesus unto him, "Go and do thou likewise."

God is not impressed by how "good" (Matthew 19:17) we think we are, but by how bad we know we are (Romans 3:23) and our willingness to seek His help to improve (1 John 1:9).

<u>Matthew 19:17</u> And Jesus said to him, "Why call Me good? There is none good but one, that is God ...

**Romans 3:23** _For all have sinned and come short of the glory of God._

**1 John 1:9** _If we confess our sins, He is faithful and just to forgive us our sins, and to cleanse us from_ _all_ _unrighteousness._

Counterfeit Christians want healed not the healer; want the gift not the giver (Acts 8:19-21), **want the miracle-working** _Savior not the loving, preventive-teaching Lord_ (John 6:26, Matthew 12:38-39)

**Acts 8:19-21 TLB** _"Let me have this power too," he exclaimed, "so that when I lay my hands on people, they will receive the Holy Spirit!" But Peter replied, "Your money perish with you for thinking God's gift can be bought!" You can have no part in this, for your heart is not right before God._

**John 6:26 TLB** _Jesus replied, "The truth of the matter is that you want to be with Me because I fed you, not because you believe in me."_

**Matthew 12:38-39 TLB** _One day some of the Jewish leaders, including some Pharisees, came to see Jesus asking to see a miracle to prove that He really was the Messiah. But Jesus replied, "Only an evil faithless nation would ask for further proof; and none will be given except what happened to Jonah the prophet! For as Jonah was in the sea monster for three days and three nights, so I, the Son of Mankind, shall be in the heart of the earth three days and three nights._

Contentment doesn't need outer circumstances to be joyous. When contentment is not influenced by worldly things, then Christian maturity is achieved. Much of content or discontent is perceived.

__Philippines 4:12-13 TLB__ I know how to live on almost nothing or with everything. I have learned the secret of contentment in every situation, whether it be a full stomach or hunger; plenty or want. For I can do everything God asks me to with the help of Christ who gives me the strength and power.

__1 Timothy 6:6__ But godliness with contentment is great gain.

How we view suffering is essential to our spiritual growth. Patient endurance (faith) can sustain itself on the conviction (belief) that hardships (bad things to good people) are not meaningless (Romans 8:28, 1 Peter 3:17), but that God will produce positive results for us even beyond our understanding. Thus, our faith will increase causing the pain to become bearable. (1 Corinthians 10:13, 1 Peter 4:1, Peter 5:9-10, Psalms 30:5) If we see no reason for our pain, we become rebellious toward God, and the pain increases. Complain and remain or praise and be raised. (1 Peter 5:10)

If a stranger walked up to you outside the convenience store, and said, "Run 10 laps around the block," you would question the motive and necessity. But, if your basketball coach said, "Run 10 laps," you would without question believing he has a good reason and goal for you.

__Romans 8:28__ And we know that all things work together for good to them that love God, to them who are called according to His purpose.

__1 Peter 3:17 TLB__ Remember, if God wants you to suffer, it is better to suffer for doing good than for doing wrong!

__1 Corinthians 10:13 TLB__ There has no temptation taken you but such is common to man. But God is faithful to keep the temptation from becoming so strong that you can't stand up *against it; but will with the temptation also make a way to escape, that you will be able to bear it.*

1 Peter 4:1 TLB Since Christ suffered and underwent pain, you must have the same attitude He did; you must be ready to suffer, too. For remember, when your body suffers, sin loses its power.

Psalms 30:5 For His anger endures but a moment; but His favor lasts a lifetime: weeping may endure for a night, but joy comes in the morning.

1 Peter 5:9-10 TLB Stand firm when he attacks. Trust the Lord; and remember that other Christians all over the world are going through these sufferings too. After you have suffered awhile, our God, who is full of kindness through Christ, will give you His eternal glory. He personally will pick you up, and set you firmly in place, and make you stronger than ever.

Joy, not rooted in the soil of suffering, is shallow.

Colossians 1:11 TLB We are praying too, that you will be filled with His mighty, glorious strength so that you can keep going no matter what happens- always full of the joy of the Lord.

Don't focus on the distasteful, focus on the dessert. Set your sights on the heavenly winner's circle, not on the earthly obstacle course.

2 Corinthians 4:18 While we look not at the things that are seen, but at the things which are not seen: for the things which are seen are temporal; but the things which are not seen are eternal.

Jesus, "the Searcher of Hearts," sees us not for whom we are, but for whom we can be. (1 Samuel 16:7). God accepts us as we are, but loves us too much not to change us. (Acts 9:1-6)

Your life may appear to be just another thorn bush until you allow God to let the rose bloom. Then people no longer focus on the thorns, but fixate on the rose's beauty.

1 Samuel 16:7 TLB But the Lord said unto Samuel, "Don't judge by his appearance or height, for I have rejected him. The Lord doesn't make decisions the way you do! People judge by outward appearance, but the Lord looks at the heart.

Acts 9:1-6 TLB But Paul threatening with every breath and eager to destroy every Christian, went to the High Priest in Jerusalem. He requested a letter addressed to synagogues in Damascus, requiring their cooperation in the persecution of any Christians he found there, both men and women, so that he could bring them in chains to Jerusalem. As he was nearing Damascus on this mission, suddenly, a brilliant light from heaven spotted down upon him. He fell to the ground and heard a voice saying to him, "Saul, Saul! Why are you persecuting Me?" "Who is speaking, sir?" Paul asked. And the voice replied, "I am Jesus, the one you are persecuting. Now get up and go into the city and await My further instructions."

Angry at Jesus

For those who are <u>mad</u> at Jesus, <u>angry</u> at Jesus or even <u>hate</u> Him, I ask you these questions:

When Jesus was exceedingly sorrowful even unto death, when in such agony that His sweat was as great drops of blood, when His best friends couldn't stay awake to pray for Him, He suffered all this as He prepared to die for your sins.

If you were there, would you have said to Him, "Let not your heart be troubled, Jesus?" He said it to you. (John 14:1)

Would you have assured Him by promising Him, "Lo, I am with you always, even unto the end of the world?" He said it to you. (Matthew 28:20)

Would you have comforted Him with the bold words, "Fear not?" He said it to you many, many times. (Luke 12:6-7)

When His heart was broken because the ones He loved rejected Him (1 Peter 5:7) would you have said, "Cast your cares on me, for I care for you?" He said it to you.

What have you done for Jesus that compares with His rejected nail-scarred hands, crown of thorns, broken heart, and flesh-tearing stripes? (Isaiah 53: 5-6)

As you hang on your self-righteous cross, have you forgiven Jesus for His love, grace, and mercy? (Luke 23:34)

Please ask yourself the question again why you are mad, angry, or hate the "Maker of the Stars" who painfully died for you rather than live without you. (John 3:19-20)

__John 14:1__ Let not your heart be troubled: you believe in God, believe also in me.

__Matthew 28:20__ Teaching them to observe all things whatsoever I have commanded you: and, lo I am with you always, even to the end of the world. Amen

__Luke 12:6-7__ Are not five sparrows sold for two pennies, and not one of them is forgotten before God? But even the very hairs of your head are all numbered. Fear not therefore: you are of more value than many sparrows.

__1 Peter 5:7__ Casting all your care upon Him for He cares for you.

Isaiah 53:5-6 (Written over 700 years before Jesus's birth) He was wounded for our transgressions, He was bruised for our iniquities: the chastisement of our peace was upon him; and with His stripes are we healed.

Luke 23:34 Then said Jesus, "Father, forgive them; for they know not what they do. And they parted His raiment, and cast lots.

John 3:19-20 And this is the condemnation, that Light is come into the world, and men loved darkness rather than light, because their deeds were evil. For every one that does evil hates the light, neither comes to the light, lest his deeds should be exposed.

We angrily disagree with God because we do not understand His ways, (Romans 11:33-34) but God faithfully loves us despite understanding our ways. (Romans 5:8)

Romans 11:33-34 Oh the depth of the riches both of the wisdom and knowledge of God! How unsearchable are His judgments, and His ways past finding out! For who has known the mind of the Lord; or who has been His counselor.

Romans 5:8 God commanded His love toward us, in that, while we were yet sinners, Christ died for us.

Who has the greater right: you to be disappointed with God, or God to be disappointed with you? (Luke 23:34, Romans 3:23, 1 Peter 1:18-19) How you judge Jesus determines how Jesus will judge you (Matthew 7:1, Matthew 10:33).

Luke 23:34 Then Jesus said, "Father, forgive them for they know not what they do."

Romans 3:23 For all have sinned and come short of the glory of God.

1 Peter 1:18-19 TLB God paid a ransom to save you from the impossible road to heaven your forefathers tried to take; and the ransom He paid was not mere gold or silver, as you very well know, but He paid for you with the precious lifeblood of Christ, the sinless, spotless Lamb of God.

Matthew 7:1 Judge not, that you be not judged.

Matthew 10:33 But whosoever shall deny Me before man, him will I deny before My Father which is in heaven.

We question God's faithfulness (Matthew 28:20), as we justify our unfaithfulness (Luke 16:15). Do not let imperfection question perfection.

Matthew 28:20 ... and, lo, I am with you always even unto the end of the world.

Luke 16:15 TLB He said unto them, "You wear a noble, pious expression in public, but God knows your evil hearts. Your pretense brings you honor from the people, but it is an abomination in the sight of God.

Jesus doesn't change us to love us; He changes us because He loves us. (John 10:10) If Jesus didn't think you could change, would He have died a painful death to cover your sins and offer you another chance? (John 8:7, 10-11)

John 10:10 The thief comes not but to steal, kill, and destroy: I am come that they might have life, and that they may have it more abundantly.

John 8:7,10-11 **Her accusers kept demanding an answer, so He stood up again and said unto them, "He that is without sin among you, let him cast the first stone at her. Then Jesus stood up again and said to her, "Where are your accusers? Didn't even one of them condemn you?" "No, sir," she said. And Jesus said, "Neither do I. Go and sin no more."**

The goal is not to get you into heaven, but to get heaven into you.

John 14:20 **At that day you shall know that I am in the Father, and you in Me and I in you.**

John 10:10 **The thief comes not but to steal, kill, and destroy: I am come that they might have life, and that they may have it more abundantly.**

John 15:4 **Abide in me and I in you. As the branch cannot bear fruit by itself, except it abide in the vine: no more can you, except you abide in me.**

Returning to her only son's intensive care room where the youngster was dying, the mother was met in the hallway by a nurse. The nurse sadly announced, "Your son is delirious and losing consciousness. He is now saying he hears angels' singing."

The grief-stricken mother replied. "I told him when the pain gets so severe that you can't bear it anymore, you will hear the angels sing."

1 Corinthians 10:13 **There has no temptation taken you but such is common to man: but God is faithful, who will not suffer you to be tempted above that you are able; but will with the temptation also make a way to escape, that you may be able to escape it.**

<u>Luke 22:43-44</u> And there appeared an angel unto Jesus from heaven, strengthening Him. And being in agony He prayed more earnestly: and His sweat was as it were great drops of blood falling down to the ground.

<u>2 Corinthians 12:9</u> And he said unto me, My grace is sufficient for you: for my strength is made perfect in weakness. Most gladly, therefore, will I rather glory in my infirmities, that the power of Christ may rest upon me.

It is not as important how you say "Hello" to life, as how you say "Good-bye." Teaching children how to live is essential; teaching them how to die is eternal.

<u>Colossians 1:28</u> Whom we preach warning every man, and teaching every man in the wisdom; that we may present every man perfect in Christ Jesus.

<u>Matthew 21:28-31 TLB</u> But what do you think about this? A man with two sons told the older boy, "Son, go out and work on the farm today." "I won't," he answered. But, later he changed his mind and went. Then the father told the youngest, "You go!", and he said, "Yes, sir I will." But, he didn't. Which of the two was obeying his father? They replied, "The first of course."

<u>Matthew 24:13</u> But he that shall endure to the end, the same shall be saved.

<u>Romans 6:16-17</u> Know you not that to whom you yield yourselves servants to obey, his servants you are to whom you obey; whether of sin unto death, or obedience unto righteousness.

A dying unchurched man, who earlier that day, had been diagnosed with terminal aggressive cancer, was visited by a minister. As the minister leaned over the bed, the burly man reached up, grabbed him by the shirt, pulled him down, and desperately said, "I know how to live, tell me how to die."

2 Corinthians 6:2 TLB For God says, "Your cry came to me at a favorable time when the doors of welcome were wide open. I helped you on a day when salvation was being offered. Right now God is ready to welcome you. Now is the day of salvation.

Philippians 1:21,24 For to me to live is Christ, and to die is gain. Nevertheless to abide in the flesh is more useful to you.

Philippians 4:12 TLB I know how to live with almost nothing or with everything. I have learned the secret of contentment in every situation, whether it be full stomach or hunger, plenty or want. I shall do all things through Christ which strengthens me.

Parents should be historians; teaching their children the spiritual successes of life.

John 9:25 He answered and said, "Whether He be a sinner or not, I know not. One thing I know, that, whereas I once was blind, now I see."

John 11:25-26 Jesus said unto her, "I am the resurrection and the life. He that believeth in Me, though he were dead, yet shall he live. And whosoever lives and believes in Me shall never die. Do you believe this?"

John 20:25-28 The other disciples said to Thomas, "We have seen the Lord." But he said to them, "Except I shall see in His hands the nail wounds and put my finger into the nail wounds, and thrust my hand into His side, I will not believe." And after eight days again His disciples were within, and Thomas with them: then came Jesus, the doors being shut, and stood in the midst, and said, "Peace be to you." Then said Jesus to Thomas, "Reach hither your finger and behold my hands: and reach hither your hand and thrust it into my side; and be not faithless, but believing. Then Thomas answered and said to Him, "My Lord and my God."

The <u>saddest eternal tragedy</u>; *For God to say, "You never understood how much I loved you since many tears ago."*

<u>**John 3:16**</u> *For God so loved (insert your name) the world that He gave His only begotten Son that whosoever believeth on Him shall not perish, but have everlasting life.*

<u>**Romans 5:8 TLB**</u> *But God showed His great love for us by sending Christ to die for us while we were yet sinners.*

<u>**Luke 23:32-34**</u> *Two other criminals were led out to be executed with Jesus at a place called "The Skull." There all three were crucified- Jesus on the center cross, and the two criminals on each side. "Father, forgive them for they know not what they do." And the soldiers gambled for His clothing, throwing dice for each piece.*

Resisting the Holy Spirit is like forming a callus. At first it hurts, but the more times you reject God, the bigger the callus and the lesser the pain.

<u>**Mark 10:17, 21-22**</u> *And when He was gone forth into the way, there came one running and kneeled before Him, and asked Him, "Good Master, what shall I do to inherit eternal life? Then Jesus looking upon him loved him and said to him, "One thing you lack: go thy way, sell whatsoever thou hast, and give to the poor, and thou shall have treasure in heaven: and come take up*

the cross and follow me." And, he was very sad at that saying, and went away grieved for he had great possessions.

Mark 8:17-18 TLB Jesus realized what they were discussing and said, "No, that isn't it at all! Can't you understand? Are your hearts too hard to take it in? As Isaiah declared, Your eyes are to see with. Why don't you look? Why don't you open your ears and listen? Don't you remember anything at all?"

Old Testament Law is like an X-ray. As we see our physical problems from an x-ray so we see from the Law our spiritual sins (Romans 7:7), but the X-ray can't cure us, and the law can't save us. God's grace heals us.

Romans 7:7 TLB Well, then am I suggesting these laws of God are evil? Of course not! No, the law is not sinful, but it was the law that showed me my sin. I would never have known the sin in my heart- the evil desires that are hidden there- if the law had not said, "You must not have evil desires in your heart.

Ephesians 2:8-9 For by grace are you saved through faith; and that not of yourselves: it is the gift of God. Not by works, lest any man should boast.

God's grace does not remove the Law; it pays the penalty.

Romans 5:20 Moreover the law entered, that the offence might abound. But where sin abounded, grace did much more abound.

There are no DIY (Do It Yourself) Christians.

Matthew 19:25-26 When His disciples heard it, they were exceedingly amazed, saying, "Who then can be saved?" But

Jesus looked at them and said unto them, "With men this is impossible; but with God all things are possible."

Obedience to God is never a Christian's option. Personal Christian revival will not come with part-time obedience.

John 14:21 He that hath My commandments and keeps them, he it is that loves Me. And he that loves Me shall be loved of my Father, and I will love him and reveal Myself to him.

Revelation 3:16 So then because you are lukewarm and neither cold nor hot, I will spit you out of my mouth.

A travelling evangelist was holding nightly services at a country church. One night as service was ending, a distressed young man came to the evangelist begging, "I must have Jesus! What must I do?"

The evangelist, recognizing the young man from previous services, said, "Across the road is a pig pen. Go wallow in the stinking manure and mud with the pigs and you shall be saved."(Mark 10:21-22) The young man shook his head, "No," and walked away knowing what people would say (John 12:43) if he did what the minister asked.

After the next night's service, the same desperate young man asked the same question with more urgency. The preacher gave the same answer with the young man giving the same response too proud to wallow with pigs. (Matthew 16:24). The next night's service was the last one, and again, the same young man came after the service pleading with the minister saying, "I MUST have Jesus come into my troubled heart. I can't live this way anymore." Again, the minister told him he needed to wallow with the pigs across the road. Desperate for a loving and forgiving Savior to cleanse his heart, the young man turned and started across the road to the filthy, stinking pig pen. As he started to climb over the gate into the pen, the minister said, "That's far enough." (Genesis 22:9-12)

<u>John 12:43</u> For they loved the praise of men more than the praise of God.

<u>Mark 10:21-22</u> Then Jesus beholding him loved him and said unto him, "One thing you lack; go your way, sell what you have, and give to the poor, and you shall have treasure in heaven: and come, take up your cross and follow Me." And he was sad at that saying, and went away grieved: for he had great possessions.

<u>Matthew 16:24</u> Then said Jesus unto His disciples, "If any man will come after Me, let him deny himself, and take up his cross and follow Me.

<u>Genesis 22:9-12</u> And they came to a place which God had told him of; and Abraham built an alter there, and laid the wood in order, and bound Isaac his son, and laid him upon the alter upon the wood. And Abraham stretched forth his hand, and took the knife to slay his son. And the angel of the Lord called unto him out of heaven, and said, "Abraham, Abraham," and he said, "Here am I." The angel said, "Lay not thy hand upon the lad, neither do anything unto him: for now I know that you fear God, seeing you have not withheld your son, your only son from Me."

Do not let anything (intelligence, money, fame, friends, blessings, toys) come between you and God. Eventually you will reap the fruits in what you put your faith.

<u>John 12:43</u> For they loved the praise of men more than the praise of God.

1 Corinthians 3:18-20 Let no man deceive himself. If any man among you seems to be wise in this world, let him become a fool, that he may be wise. For the wisdom of this world is foolishness with God. For it is written, God uses man's own brilliance to trap him. He stumbles over his own "wisdom" and falls. And again the Lord knows the thoughts of the wise and they are vain.

Romans 14:23 TLB Anyone who believes that something he wants is to do is wrong, shouldn't do it. He sins if he does, for he thinks it is wrong and for him it is wrong. For whatsoever is not of faith is sin.

Matthew 6:21 For where your treasure is, there will your heart be also.

As God's spirit convicts and you truly encounter Jesus, you become **spiritually nude.** As all heavy-burdened schemes, lies, excuses, psychological defenses, and face-saving techniques melt, Jesus washes all your burdens away and clothes you with loving righteousness.

Psalms 51:7 TLB Purify me from my sins, and I will be clean; wash me and I will be whiter than snow.

Isaiah 61:10 I will greatly rejoice in the Lord, my soul shall be joyful in my God; for He hath clothed me with the garments of salvation, He has covered me with the robe of righteousness, as a bridegroom decks himself with ornaments, and as a bride adorns herself with her jewels.

When life is fading, one realizes that only three things matter: who loves you; who you love; and your relationship with Jesus Christ.

John 15:9 As the Father has loved Me, so have I loved you: continue in My love.

John 13:1 Now before the feast of the Passover, when Jesus knew that His hour was come that He should depart out of this world unto the Father, having loved His own which were in the world, He loved them unto the end.

John 21:17 TLB He said unto him the third time, "Simon, son of John, are you even My friend?" Peter was grieved at the way Jesus asked the question the third time. "Lord, you know my heart, You know I am." Jesus said, "Then feed My sheep."

Luke 23:34 Then said Jesus, "Father forgive them; for they know not what they do. And they parted his raiment, and cast lots.

If you live long enough, there will come a time when for God to answer your prayer will mean more to you than anything in the world.

Psalms 55:2 TLB Please listen and answer me, for I am overwhelmed by my troubles.

James 5:15 TLB Their prayer, if offered in faith, will heal him, for the Lord will make him well; and if his sickness was caused by some sin, the Lord will forgive him.

1 Peter 3:12 For the eyes of the Lord are over the righteous, and His ears are open to their prayers: but the face of the Lord is against them that do evil.

Spiritually, comfort the afflicted; afflict the comfortable.

Matthew 5:5 Blessed are the meek for they shall inherit the earth.

Matthew 25:45 Then shall He answer them saying, "Verily I say unto you, inasmuch as you did it not unto one of the least of these, you did it not unto me.

(Procrastination) To avoid doing "good" when such is within one's power is to do harm.

__James 4:17__ Therefore, to him that knows to do good, and doesn't do it, to him it is a sin.

A nation's greatness lies in *Godly parents* and *Prayer Warriors* who are never too young or too old to serve God.

__Proverbs 22:6__ Train up a child in the way he should go, and when he is old, he will not depart from it.

__Colossians 4:12__ Epaphras, who is one of you, a servant of Christ, salutes you always laboring fervently for you in prayers, that you may stand perfect and complete in all the will of God.

__1 Timothy 2:1 TLB__ Here are my directions: pray much for others; plead for God's mercy upon them; give thanks for all He is going to do for them.

__2 Chronicles 7:14__ If My people which are called by My name shall __humble__ themselves, and __pray__, and __seek__ My face, and __turn__ from their wicked ways; then will I hear from heaven, and forgive their sin, and __will heal their land.__

When a mighty warrior met another soldier who was being eulogized, he would ask, "Show me your scars?" No scars, no warrior. Wounds are not as glorious as scars (healed wounds). Sadly, some spiritual wounds are never allowed to heal by those who have them.

__Galatians 6:17 TLB__ From now on please don't argue with me about these things, for I carry on my body the scars of the whippings and wounds from Jesus' enemies that mark me as His slave.

Romans 14:12 So then every one of us shall give an account of himself to God.

Matthew 5:11-12 Blessed are you when men shall revile you, and persecute you, and shall say all manner of evil against you falsely for my name sake. Rejoice and be exceedingly glad: for great is your reward in heaven: for persecuted the prophets which were before you.

The gospel is free, but you must pay for the plumbing. You must give your life to God for the gospel to flow through you.

Matthew 10:39 He that finds his life shall lose it, and he that loses his life for My sake shall find it.

It's not the battle one should fear, but choosing the right captain.

Ephesians 6: 12 TLB For we are not fighting against people made of flesh and blood, but against persons without bodies, the evil rulers of the unseen world, those mighty satanic beings and great evil princes of darkness who rule the world; and against huge numbers of wicked spirits in the spirit world.

II Peter 2:19 TLB "You aren't saved by being good," they say, "so you might as well be bad. Do what you like, be free." But these very teachers who offer this "freedom" from the law are themselves slaves to sin and destruction. For a man is a slave to whatever controls him.

Romans 6:16 TLB Don't you realize you can choose your own master? You can choose sin (with death) or else obedience (with acquittal). The one to whom you offer yourself- he will take you and be your master and you will be his slave.

Either you are a thermometer (Life controls you) or a thermostat (You control life).

Joshua 24:15 And if it seem evil unto you to serve the Lord, choose you this day whom you will serve ... But as for me and my house, we will serve the Lord.

James 1:6 But let him ask in faith, not wavering. For he that wavers is like a wave of the sea driven with the wind and tossed.

My neighbor, Ron, who is a devoted Christian, called telling me he and his wife, Jennifer, were driving home yesterday when an oncoming car came into their lane forcing them into the ditch and overturning their car. Jennifer, who is now out of intensive care, is steadily recovering. Ron wanted to know if I would drive him to his car to get some of their belongings.

When we arrived, Ron's car was in a lot with dozens of other damaged vehicles. After seeing their car, I remarked how lucky Jennifer and Ron were that no one was killed. Ron agreed and told me that when he called the other driver to hear how he was getting along, he was told he had no insurance. Fortunately for Ron's family they had total coverage even for uninsured motorist.(2 Thessalonians 3:2-3) Ron is a wonderful driver who has never had an accident or even a ticket, but even good drivers get into accidents, even accidents caused by themselves. (Romans 3:10)

When we look at human lives whether Christian or not, we see sickness, death, job loss, pain, tears, and other tragedies. Although concerned about Jennifer, I could tell how relieved Ron was to have insurance to cover all expenses involved with the accident.

We may not be able to identify the Christians from those who are not by the tragedies in their lives, but we can tell the Christians (those insured) by how they handle the tragedies (II Corinthians 12:10, John 16:33, John 17:15).

When looking through a junkyard, can you tell which vehicles were insured and which weren't? (Matthew 5:45)

Everyone (Romans 3:23, 1 John 1:10) falls into one of two kinds of natural-born (Romans 5:12) sinners, Rescued (1 Peter 3:12) or Non-rescued (Psalms 66:18, Proverbs 28:9). The Rescued are righteous because they are under warranty. All insurer's damage (sin) is under warranty so the cost has been paid. (1 Peter 3:18)

Non-rescued may have same (sin) damage, but since they are not under warranty, they are, by their own choosing, self-insured. (Romans 6:23)

__2 Thessalonians 3:2-3 TLB__ Pray too that you will be saved out of the clutches of evil men, for not everyone loves the Lord. But the Lord is faithful; He will make you strong and guard you from satanic attacks of every kind.

__Romans 3:10__ As it is written; there is none righteous, no, not one.

__2 Corinthians 12:10__ Therefore, I take pleasure in infirmities, in reproaches, in necessities, in persecutions, in distresses for Christ's sake: for when I am weak, then am I strong.

__John 16:33, 17:15__ These things have I spoken unto you that in me you might have peace. In the world you shall have tribulation: but be of good cheer for I have overcome the world. I pray that thou should not take them out of the world, but thou should keep them from the evil.

Matthew 5:45 *That you may be the children of your Father which is in heaven: for He makes His sun to rise on the evil and on the good and sends rain on the just and on the unjust.*

Romans 3:23 *For all have sinned and come short of the glory of God.*

1 John 1:10 *If we say we have not sinned, we make Him a liar, and His word is not in us.*

Romans 5:12 *Wherefore, as by one man sin entered into the world; and death by sin; and so death passed upon all men, for that all have sinned.*

1 Peter 3:12 *For the eyes of the Lord are over the righteous, and His ears are open unto their prayers: but the face of the Lord is against them that do evil.*

Psalms 66:18 *If I regard iniquity in my heart, the Lord will not hear me.*

Proverbs 28:9 TLB *The prayers of the person who ignores the law are despised.*

1 Peter 3:18 TLB *Christ also suffered. He died once for the sins of all us guilty sinners, although He Himself was innocent of any sin at any time that he might bring us safely home to God. But though His body died, His spirit lived on.*

Romans 6:23 *For the wages of sin is death; but the gift of God is eternal life through Jesus Christ our Lord.*

There is a difference between saying someone is a great teacher and passing that teacher's class.

Mark 10: 17, 21-22 As He was starting out on a trip, a man came running to Him, and knelt down and asked, "Good Teacher what must I do to get to heaven?"Jesus felt genuine love for the man as He looked at him. "You lack only one thing," He told him, "go and sell all you have and give the money to the poor, and you will have treasure in heaven, and come, follow me." Then the man's face fell, and he went sadly away, for he was very rich.

It's easy to tell which people have problems. They're breathing.

Romans 3:23 For all have sinned and come short of the glory of God.

When dying of thirst, don't ask for a candy bar.

Matthew 12:38-39 Then certain of the scribes and of the Pharisees answered, saying, "Master, show us a sign from Thee." But, he answered and said to them, "An evil and adulterous generation seeks after a sign; and there no sign shall be given to it, but the sign of the prophet Jonah."

John 4:10 Jesus answered and said unto her, "If you had known the gift of God, and who it is that said to you, give me a drink, you would have asked of Him and He would have given you living water."

Hebrews 11:25 Choosing rather to suffer the affliction with the people of God than to enjoy the fleeting pleasures of sin for a season.

Matthew 12:38-39 TLB One day some of the Jewish leaders, including some Pharisees, came to see Jesus asking to see a miracle to prove that He really was the Messiah. But Jesus replied, "Only an evil faithless nation would ask for further proof; and none will be given except what happened to Jonah the prophet! For as Jonah was in the sea monster for three days and three nights, so I, the Son of Mankind, shall be in the heart of the earth three days and three nights.

Every sin verifies the need for a Savior.

Romans 3: 23-25 TLB All have sinned and come short of the glory of God. Yet now God declares us "not guilty" of offending Him, if we trust in Jesus Christ, who in His kindness freely takes away our sins. For God sent Christ Jesus to take the punishment for our sins and to end all God's anger against us. He used Christ's blood and our faith as the means of saving us from His wrath …

Romans 6:23 For the wages of sin is death; but the gift of God is eternal life through Jesus Christ, our Lord.

Hebrews 9:22 And almost all things are by the law purged with blood; and without the shedding of blood there is no forgiveness of sins.

Sin is one of the fruits of humanity's free-will.

Genesis 3: 2-3,6 And the woman said unto the serpent, "We may eat of the fruit of the trees of the garden; but the fruit of the tree which is in the midst of the garden, God has said, 'you shall not eat of it, neither shall you touch it, lest you die.'" And when the woman saw the tree was good for food, and that it was pleasant to the eyes, and a tree to be desired to make one wise, she took of the fruit thereof, and did eat, and gave also unto her husband with her, sand he did eat.

Galatians 5:19-21 TLB But when you follow your own wrong inclinations, your lives will produce these evil results: impure thoughts, eagerness for lustful pleasure, idolatry, spiritism (encouraging the activity of demons), hatred and fighting, jealousy, anger, constant effort to get the best for yourself, complaints and criticism, the feeling everyone else is wrong except those in your own little group- and there will be wrong doctrine. Envy murder, drunkenness, wild parties, and all that sort of thing. Let me tell you again as I have before that anyone living that sort of life will not inherit the kingdom of God.

The easiest sins to confess are the sins of others.

<u>1 John 1:9</u> If we confess <u>our</u> sins, He is faithful and just to forgive us our sins, and to cleanse us from all unrighteousness.

<u>Matthew 7:3 TLB</u> And why worry about a speck in the eye of a brother when you have a board in your own eye.

What are bad events? Who determines if something bad happens to "good" people? (John 11:14, John 12:9 John 9: 1-3, Romans 8:28) Suffering can be a blessing. (I Peter 4: 1, 12-14) If bad things happen to good people, why is the crucifixion called, "Good Friday?" (Luke 23:46) And, if the crucifixion Friday is called "good," how should the resurrection Sunday be described?

<u>John 11:14, 44</u> Then said Jesus to them plainly, "Lazarus is dead." And Lazarus that was dead came forth, bound hand and foot with grave clothes: and his face was bound about with a napkin. Jesus said, "Loose him and let him go."

<u>John 12:9</u> Much of the Jews therefore, knew that He was there, and they came not for Jesus' sake only, but that they might see Lazarus also, whom He had raised from the dead.

John 9:1-3 And as Jesus passed by, He saw a man which was blind from birth. And His disciples asked Him, saying, "Master, who did sin, this man or his parents that he was born blind?" Jesus answered, "Neither has this man sinned or his parents: but that the works of God should be displayed in him."

Romans 8:28 And we know that all things work together for good to them that love God, to them who are called according to His purpose.

1 Peter 4:1,12-14 TLB Since Christ suffered and underwent pain, you must have the same attitude He did; you must be ready to suffer, too. For when your body suffers, sin loses its power. Beloved think it not strange concerning the fiery trial which are to try you, as though some strange thing happened to you. But rejoice inasmuch as you are partakers of Christ's sufferings; that when His glory shall be revealed, you may be glad also with exceeding joy. If you suffer for the name of Christ, happy are you for the Spirit of glory and of God rests on you: on their part He is blasphemed, but on your part He is glorified.

Luke 23:46 And when Jesus had cried with a loud voice, He said, "Father into your hands I commend My spirit.' And having said thus, He gave up the ghost.

If you were there in the crowd knowing that your only way to heaven was Jesus' death, through your tears would you shout, "Crucify Him?"

John 19:5-6 Then came Jesus forth wearing the crown of thorns, and the purple robe. And Pilate said to them, "Behold the man!" When the chief priests therefore and officers saw Him, they cried out, "Crucify Him, Crucify Him." Pilate said to them, "You take Him and crucify Him; for I find no fault in Him."

<u>Hebrews 9:22</u> And almost all things are by the law purged with blood; and without shedding of blood is no remission.

A woman with a vulture on her head, a banana in her ear, and a carrot up her nose walks into the psychiatrist's office and says, "I'm here about my neighbor."

<u>Matthew 7: 4</u> How will you say to your brother, "Let me pull the speck out of your eye," and, behold, a beam is in your own eye.

Like a loving parent, God is more often disappointed than angry.

<u>Matthew 23:37</u> O Jerusalem, Jerusalem, thou that kills the prophets, and stones them which are sent to you, how often would I have gathered your children together, even as a hen gathers her chickens under her wings, and you would not.

<u>Luke 23:21,34</u> But they shouted, "Crucify Him! Crucify Him!" Then Jesus said, "Father, forgive them; for they know not what they do. And they parted His raiment, and cast lots.

God has no grandchildren just children. Christian parents' faiths do not guarantee their children to be heaven bound, and neither do unbelieving parents assure their children to be hell bound.

<u>Matthew 5:45</u> That you may be the children of your Father which is in heaven: for He makes His sun to rise on the evil and on the good, and sends rain on the just and on the unjust.

<u>Romans 2:28-29 TLB</u> For you are not real Jews just because you were born of Jewish parents or because you have gone through the Jewish initiation ceremony of circumcision. No a real Jew is anyone whose heart is right with God. God is not looking for those who cut their bodies in actual circumcision, but He is

looking for those with changed hearts and minds. Whoever has that kind of change in his life will get his praise from God, even if not from you.

<u>*Romans 8:16*</u> *The Spirit itself bears witness with our spirit, that we are the children of God.*

Disappointment is an ingredient of love. One of the frequent causes of pain is love.

<u>*Luke 19:41-42*</u> *As they came closer to Jerusalem and He saw the city ahead, He began to cry. "Eternal peace was within your reach and you turned it down," He wept, "and now it is too late."*

<u>*John 11:35-36*</u> *Jesus wept. Then said the Jews, "Behold how He loved him!"*

The God that created "free will" is not the problem, but what decisions we make with this gift can be. The Tree of Knowledge of Good and Evil was hurting no one. It wasn't the "apple" on the tree that was the problem, but the pair (pear!) on the ground!

<u>*Genesis 2:17, 3:6*</u> *But the tree of the knowledge of good and evil you shall not eat of it; for in the day that you eat thereof, you shall surely die. And when the woman saw that the tree was good for food, and it was pleasant to the eyes, and a tree to be desired to make one wise, she took of the fruit thereof, and did eat and gave also to her husband with her, and he did eat.*

Mankind has always had free-will (Genesis 2:17, Genesis 3:6, Joshua 24:15, John 3:16). With free-will there must be a choice and with the choices there must be different results (Revelation 20: 12, Revelation 21: 3-4). Because there is a place (heaven) for those wanting to be with Jesus, the author of every good and perfect gift (James 1:17), there must be a place (hell) for those rejecting to faithfully follow Him (Revelation 20:15).

__Genesis 2:17, 3:6__ But the tree of the knowledge of good and evil you shall not eat of it; for in the day that you eat thereof, you shall surely die. And when the woman saw that the tree was good for food, and it was pleasant to the eyes, and a tree to be desired to make one wise, she took of the fruit thereof, and did eat and gave also to her husband with her, and he did eat.

__Joshua 24:15 TLB__ But if you are unwilling to serve the Lord, then choose today whom you will serve. Would you prefer the gods of your ancestors served beyond the Euphrates? Or will it be the gods of the Amorites in whose land you now live? But as for me and my house, we will serve the Lord.

__John 3:16__ For God so loved the world that He gave His only begotten Son; that whosoever believes in Him should not perish, but have everlasting life.

__Revelation 20:12__ And I saw the dead both small and great stand before God; and the books were opened: and another book was opened which is the book of life: and the dead were judged out of those things which were written in the books, according to their works.

__Revelation 21:3-4__ And I heard a great voice out of heaven saying, "Behold the tabernacle of God is with men and He will dwell with them, and they shall be His people, and God Himself shall be with them, and be their God.

__James 1:17__ Every good and every perfect gift is from above, and comes down from the Father of lights, with whom is no variableness, neither shadow of turning.

Revelation 20:15 And whoever was not found written in the book of life was cast into the lake of fire.

Mankind's greatest eternal decision: Keep sin and ask Jesus to leave, or keep Jesus and ask sin to leave.

Matthew 8:34 And behold the whole city came out to meet Jesus, and when they saw Him, they begged Him that He would depart out of their coasts.

Jonah 3:10 And God saw their works, that they turned from their evil way: and God had mercy on them and didn't carry out the destruction He had threatened.

Spiritually, we have a gaping amputation (separation from Jesus) that will not heal and keeps oozing (Galatians 5: 19-21). We put ineffective man-made religious and philosophical salves on it. We ignore the wound; we deny the wound. We administer drugs, sports, sex, parties, and entertainment of all sorts. We can get temporary relief but nothing cures (Hebrews 11:25). Since we have lived with it for so long, the pain at times goes unnoticed; other times it is unbearable. The wound wears us down (Matthew 11: 28-30).

Unless we heal by attaching ourselves to Jesus (Galatians 5: 22-24, we will spiritually die never reaching the heights of joy, peace, love that Jesus offers. Only Jesus can satisfy your soul. Our Savior never diminishes joy, but always enhances our lives.

Galatians 5:19-21 TLB But when you follow your own wrong inclinations, your lives will produce these evil results: impure thoughts, eagerness for lustful pleasure, idolatry, witchcraft, hatred, fighting, jealousy, anger, ... envy, murder, drunkenness, wild parties and all that sort of thing. They that do such things will not inherit the kingdom of heaven.

__Hebrews 11:25__ Choosing rather to suffer affliction with the people of God, than to enjoy the pleasures of sin for a season.

__Matthew 11:28-30__ Come to Me all you that labor and are heavy laden, and I will give you rest. Take My yoke upon you, and learn of me: for I am meek and lowly in heart, and you will find rest for your souls. For My yoke is easy, and My burden is light.

__Galatians 5:22-24 TLB__ But the fruit of the spirit is love, joy, peace, patience, kindness, goodness, faithfulness, gentleness, and self-control and here there is no conflict with Jewish laws. Those who belong to Christ have nailed their natural evil desires to His cross and crucified them there.

The saddest people in the world are those who thought worldly pleasures would last a lifetime and found that to be untrue.

__Proverbs 13:15__ Good understanding gives favor, but the way of the transgressor is hard.

__Job 4:8__ Even as I have seen, they that plow iniquity and sow wickedness, reap the same.

Are you a patient patient of patience (Isaiah 40:31, James 1:4)? Patience (endurance) is not inactive, but is learning how to "play hurt." When you pray for patience, you get tribulation, (Romans 5:3-4) just like crushing grapes gets you wine. When a Christian asks for patience, does she get "peace" or "tribulation?" The answer is "Yes."

__Isaiah 40:31__ But they that wait upon the Lord shall renew their strength; they shall mount up as wings as eagles, they shall run and not be weary; and they shall walk and not be fain.

James 1:4 Let patience have her perfect work, that you may be perfect and entire, wanting nothing.

Romans 5:3 ... We glory in tribulations also, knowing that tribulation works patience.

Satan never tells you the consequences of following him.

John 8:44 You are of your father, the devil, and the lusts of your father you will do. He is a murderer from the beginning, and abides not in the truth, because there is no truth in him. When he speaks a lie, he speaks of his own; for he is a liar and the father of liars.

Revelation 21:8 TLB Cowards who turn back from following me, and those who are unfaithful to Me, and the corrupt, and murders, and the immoral, and those conversing with demons, and idol worshipers, and all liars- their doom is in the Lake that burns with fire and sulfur. This is the second death.

If you don't want a fly swatter, then you'll have to put up with the flies.

Proverbs 13:15 Good understanding gives favor, but the way of the transgressor is hard.

When praying, whether you use the clause, "thy will be done" or not, determines if you desire your will or God's will. (Luke 11:2, Matthew 26:42). Be careful what you ask for. (Matthew 27:25)

Luke 11:2 And He said unto them, "When you pray, say, Our Father which art in heaven, hallowed be your name. Thy kingdom come, Thy will be done, as in heaven so on earth.

Matthew 26:42 He went away again the second time, and prayed, saying, "O, My Father, if this cup may not pass away from me, except I drink it, Thy will be done."

Matthew 27:25 Then answered all the people and said, "His blood be on us and on our children.

When present, "suffering," makes it difficult, but not impossible, to say "Thy will be done."

Luke 22:42, 44 Saying, "Father, if you are willing, remove this cup from Me: nevertheless, not My will, but yours be done. And being in such agony He prayed more earnestly: and His sweat was as it were great drops of blood falling down to the ground.

When you do not say to God, "Thy will be done," then God says to you *the most fearful words*, "Thy will be done."

Matthew 27: 24-25 TLB When Pilate saw that he wasn't getting anywhere, and that a riot was developing, he sent for a bowl of water and washed his hands before the crowd, saying, "I am innocent of the blood of this good man. The responsibility is yours!" And the mob yelled back, "His blood is on us and our children!"

Never fear God's will. Within the will of God is the safest place one can be.

Philippines 4: 13 I can do all things through Christ who strengthens me.

I Corinthians 10:13 There is no temptation taken you but such as is common to man: but God faithful, who will not suffer you to be tempted above that you are able; but will with the temptation also make a way to escape, that you may be able to bear it.

Which is the greater value, the cost of a three-week vacation or the cost of eternity with a loving Savior?

Philippians 3:8 TLB Everything else is worthless when compared with the priceless gain of knowing Christ Jesus my Lord. I have put aside all else, counting it worth less than nothing; in order that I can have Christ.

Luke 14: 27-28 Whosoever does not bear his cross and come after me, cannot be my disciple. For which of you intending to build a tower sits not down first and counts the cost, whether he has sufficient funds to finish it.

The time and money we devote to medicine, health care, beauty, exercise, and vitamins to live longer on this sinful earth with a decaying body (1 Corinthians 15:44) far exceeds the personal resources we devote to live with a new body eternally in heaven.

Genesis 3: 19 All your life you will sweat to produce food, until your dying day. Then you will return to the ground from which you came. For you were made from dust and to the dust you will return.

1 Corinthians 15:44 TLB They are just human bodies at death, but when they come back to life, they will be superhuman bodies. For just as there are natural, human bodies, there are also supernatural, spiritual bodies.

2 Corinthians 5:1 TLB For we know that this tent we live in now is taken down-when we die and leave these bodies-we will have wonderful new bodies in heaven, homes that will be ours forevermore, made for us by God Himself, and not by human hands.

Mark 8:36 For what shall it profit a man if he shall gain the whole world, and lose his own soul?

Revelation 21:4 And God shall wipe away all tears from their eyes; and there shall be no more death, neither sorrow, nor crying, neither shall there be any more pain; for the former things are passed away.

When praying say, "Yes, Lord, now what is the question?"

John 14:15 If you love Me, keep My commandments.

Matthew 7:21 Not everyone that says unto me, "Lord, Lord," shall enter into the kingdom of heaven, but he that does the will of My Father, which is in heaven."

Isaiah 6:8 Then I heard the voice of the Lord, saying, "Whom shall I send, and who will go for us?" Then said I, "Here am I, send me."

You can choose to go to Hell unsaved, but not unloved.

John 3:16, 18 For God so loved (substitute your name) the world that He gave His only begotten Son, that whosoever believes in Him shall not perish, but have everlasting life. He that believes on Him is not condemned, but he that believes not is condemned already, because he has not believed in the name of the only begotten Son of God.

II Peter 3:9 TLB He isn't really being slow about His promised return, even though it sometimes seems that way. But He is waiting for the good reason that He is not willing that any should perish, and He is giving more time for sinners to repent.

He is no fool who gives what he cannot keep to gain what he cannot lose.

Matthew 6:19-20 Lay not up for yourselves treasures upon earth, where moth and rust doth corrupt, and where thieves break through and steal. Lay up for yourselves treasures in heaven where neither moth nor rust corrupt, and where thieves do not break through and steal.

Mark 8: 35 For whosoever shall save his life shall lose it, but whosoever shall lose his life for My sake and the gospels, the same shall save it.

Even if you win the rat race, you're still a rat.

Mark 8: 36 For what shall it profit a man, if he shall gain the whole world, and lose his own soul?

If someone wonders how much grace God has, in any measurement, the answer is always, "Enough!"

Romans 5:20 Moreover the law entered, that the offence might abound. But where sin abounded, grace did much more abound.

There is a difference between a missionary (John 3:17) and a policeman (John 5:30).

John 3:17 For God sent not His Son into the world to condemn the world, but that the world through Him might be saved.

John 5:30 I can of My own self do nothing; as I hear, I judge and My judgment is just because I speak not My own will, but the will of the Father which sent Me.

Never doubt in the Light what you learned in the darkness.

Matthew 10: 27 What I tell you in darkness that speak you in the light. And, what you hear in the ear, that preach you on the housetops.

Isaiah 45:3 I will give you the treasures of darkness, and the hidden riches of secret places, that you may know that I, the Lord, which call you by your name, am the God of Israel.

Don't let other's opinions blur your vision.

John 9:24-25 Then called they the man that was blind and said unto him, "give God the praise. We know Jesus is a sinner." He answered and said, "Whether he be a sinner or not, I know not. One thing I know that once I was blind, now I see."

Grandma Ida's oft used prayer, "Lord, deliver me from my friends."

Mark 3:21 When His friends heard what was happening, they came to try to take Him home with them. "He is out of his mind," they said.

John 2:24-25 TLB But Jesus didn't trust them, for He knew mankind to the core. No one needed to tell Him how changeable human nature is!

Faith not tested cannot be trusted. You will not know the power of what God can do in your life without tribulation. How will you know how great a baseball pitcher is if no batter ever swings at his pitches? Or, how will you know how good a running back is if no one tries to tackle him? And how will they know how to improve to greatness if not challenged?

Mark 4:38-39 TLB Jesus was asleep at the back of the boat with His head on a cushion. Frantically they awakened Him, shouting, "Teacher, don't you even care we are all about to drown?" Then He rebuked the wind and said to the sea, "Quiet down!" and the wind fell, and there was a great calm.

Luke 22: 56-57 A certain maid beheld him as he sat by the fire, and earnestly looked upon him and said, "This man was also with Him." And he denied it saying, "Woman, I know him not."

James 1:12 Blessed is the man that endures temptation for when he is tried, he shall receive the crown of life, which the Lord has promised to those that love Him.

Isaiah 45:3 I will give you the treasures of darkness, and the hidden riches of secret places, that you may know that I, the Lord, which call you by your name, am the God of Israel.

Matthew 10:27 What I tell you in darkness, that speak you in light: and what you hear in the ear, that preach you on the rooftops.

Hypocrite says behind your back what he will not say to your face while a flatter says to your face what he will not say behind your back.

Matthew 5: 44 But I say to you love your enemies, bless them that curse you, do good to them that hate you, and pray for them that despitefully use you, and persecute you.

Matthew 15:8-9 TLB These people say they honor Me, but their hearts are far away. Their worship is worthless, for they teach their manmade laws instead of those from God.

John 2:23-25 TLB Because of the miracles He did in Jerusalem at the Passover celebration, many people were convinced that He was indeed the Messiah. But Jesus didn't trust them, for He knew mankind to the core. No one needed to tell Him how changeable human nature is.

If you talk the talk, you must walk the walk. Woe to those who confess Jesus by mouth and crucify Him with their actions.

John 19:4 Pilate went outside again and said to them, "Behold, I bring forth to you that you may know that I find no fault in Him."

Titus 1:16 TLB Such persons claim they know God, but from seeing the way they act, one knows they do not. They are rotten and disobedient, worthless so far as doing anything good is concerned.

1 John 1:6 If we say we have fellowship with Him, and walk in darkness, we lie, and do not the truth.

How you dance is not as important as the music to which you're dancing.

John 7:17 If any of you really determines to do God's will, then you will certainly know whether My teaching is from God or is merely My own.

1 John 4:1 TLB Dearly loved friends, don't always believe everything you hear just because someone says it is a message from God: test it first to see if it really is. For, there are many false teachers around.

2 Samuel 6:14-15 TLB And David danced before the Lord with all his might wearing a priestly tunic. So David and all Israel brought up the Ark of the Lord with much shouting and blowing of trumpets.

When you become a Christian, don't worry about leaving your friends, they'll leave you. (John 6:26 TLB, Luke 6:22, Luke 21:16, 1 Peter 4:4) Conversion will bring conflict. Real, true friends love you for whom you are. False friends love only your actions that please them.

Jesus replied, "The truth of the matter is that you want to be with Me because I fed you, not because you believe in Me."

Luke 6:22 Blessed are you when men shall hate you and when they shall separate you from their company, and shall denounce you and cast out your name as evil, for the Son of man's sake.

Luke 21:16-17 And, you shall be betrayed both by parents and brethren, and relatives and friends, and some of you will be killed. And you will be hated of all men for My name's sake.

1 Peter 4:4 TLB Of course, your former friends will be very surprised when you don't eagerly join them anymore in the wicked things they do, and they will laugh at you in contempt and scorn.

Love the sinner, hate the sin. (Jude 22-23) One of the differences between a girl and a woman, or a boy and a man is when one can appreciate the good qualities of another without being consumed by the bad qualities. There are 50-year-old boys and girls as well as 12-year-old men and women.

Jude 22-23 TLB Try to help those who argue against you. Be merciful to those who doubt. Save some by snatching them from the very flames of hell itself. And as for others help them to find the Lord by being kind to them, but be careful that you yourselves aren't pulled along into their sins. Hate every trace of their sin while being merciful to them as sinners.

"Compassion" can be linked with either "converting" (Mark 1:40-42) or "enabling." (John 6:26, 30-31) Jesus had compassion not for the leper, but for the man who had leprosy. The same can be said for the demon-possessed man. There will be no sin, no drugs, no diseases, no homosexuality, no demons in heaven. Often we compassionately enable homosexuality, the sexual pervert, drug addict, or morally corrupt by providing excuses and physical needs when we should be trying to remove the sin from the sinner (Philippines 4:13).

Would one compassionately comfort a screaming child with badly broken legs and not seek medical attention for her because one would feel good about pushing this child through life in a wheelchair?

The difference between a church (Mark 16:15) and a charitable organization is a church takes mankind's needs beyond the physical and adds the eternal spiritual needs as well.

Mark 1:40-42 And there came a leper to Him beseeching Him, and kneeling down to Him and saying unto Him, "If thou wilt, thou can make me clean. And Jesus moved with compassion, put forth His hand, and touched him, and said unto him, "Be thou clean." And as soon as He had spoken, immediately the leprosy departed from him and he was cleansed.

John 6:26, 30-31 TLB Jesus replied, "The truth of the matter is that you want to be with Me because I fed you, not because you believe in Me.' They replied, "You must show us more miracles if you want us to believe You are the Messiah, Give us free bread every day, like our fathers had while they journeyed through the wilderness!"

Philippines 4:13 I can do all things through Christ which strengthens me.

Mark 16:15 And He said unto them, "Go into all the world and preach the gospel to every creature."

The difference between humanitarians, who may have achieved many good works, and Christians is blood/believing. (Isaiah 64:6, Matthew 7:22-23, Romans 5:9) Good works do not produce Christian faith (Isaiah 64:6, Titus 3:5). Christian faith produces good works. Humanitarians try to make the world a better place from which to go to hell.

Isaiah 64:6 But we are all as an unclean thing, and all our righteousness are as filthy rags; and we all do fade as a leaf; and our iniquities as the wind have taken us away.

Matthew 7:22-23 Many shall say unto Me in that day, Lord, Lord, have we not prophesied in Thy name? And in Thy name have we not cast out devils; and in Thy name done many wonderful works? And then will I profess unto them, "I never knew you. Depart from Me you that do iniquity."

Romans 5:9 TLB And since by His blood He did all this for us as sinners, how much more will He do for us now that He has declared us not guilty? Now He can save us from all God's wrath to come.

__Titus 3:5__ Then He saved us Christians – but because of His kindness and pity – by washing away our sins and giving us the new joy of the indwelling Holy Spirit.

You were born an original, don't die a copy. (Ephesians 4:11) You can be like a brother or sister without being like a twin.

__Ephesians 4:11 TLB__ Some of us have been given special ability as apostles; to others He has given the gift of being able to preach well; some have special ability in winning people to Christ, helping them to trust Him as their Savior: still others have a gift for caring for God's people as a shepherd does his sheep, leading and teaching them in God's ways

Hate consumes the vessel that contains it. The same can be said of love (Luke 10:27). Note: This includes our opinion of ourselves. As a Christian, you are a gift to God (Ephesians 1:18), therefore, love the Giver and gift.

__Luke 10:27__ And He answering said, "You should love the Lord your God with all your heart and with all your soul, and with all your strength, and with all your mind; and your neighbor as yourself."

__Ephesians 1:18 TLB__ I pray that your hearts will be flooded with light so that you can see something of the future He has called you to share. I want you to know God has been made rich because we who are Christ's have been given to Him.

By chance I met a former classmate, Debbi, whom I hadn't seen in years. As we tried to "catch up" on our lives, I asked how she met her husband. She smiled fondly at his name, and stated it started with a blind date.

This fellow wanted to meet Debbi, but she was hesitant. She had heard of him and had known others who knew him (Romans 10:13-14), but had never met him personally. When a mutual friend suggested a blind date, she was a little apprehensive about such a meeting. Debbi stated she was already in a relationship, however, it was going nowhere and problems had already arisen. He was convincing and selfishly possessive. (2 Timothy 2:26)

After several pleadings from friends, Debbi decided she had nothing to lose and consented. Although the blind date was uneventful, Debbi realized the fellow was sincere and took an interest in her. There was just something about this person that caught Debbi's interest. Not being the pushy kind, this man asked Debbi if he could see her again.

Again, Debbi spoke with friends who knew him and after several requests she agreed to another date. The fact that Debbi realized she was weary in her present not-going-anywhere relationship helped her make this decision. (Matthew 11:28) They just couldn't seem to be on the same page when a concern arose. (James 4:7)

The more she met with her future husband, the more she enjoyed their time together. Her future husband helped her realize how insensitive and selfish her present friend really was.

At first there were times when her future husband would knock on her front door (Revelation 3:20), but she didn't want to see him. However, he had a gentle forgiving way of patiently calling later. The more time she spent with this new friend the more she got to know him. And, the more she got to know him the more she liked him. Over time she could not go a day without texting or seeing him. (1 Thessalonians 5:17)

Finally, she accepted his marriage proposal (John 4:23) and together they have conquered life's trials. (Matthew 11:29) The more conquered trials the closer they became. The love, joy, and peace in Debbi's life reached greater fulfillment. Although believing that love-at-first-sight can happen, Debbi believes that marriage precedes fulfilled love. She and her husband's love grew gradually and still grows continuously long after the marriage ceremony.

As the subject turned to me, and I explained my glorious walk with Jesus, which enhances everything I do, Debbi asked, "How do you start a faith in Jesus?" To my delight I exclaimed, "You just explained it wonderfully! Want to go on a blind date?"

***Romans 10:13-14 TLB** Anyone who calls upon the name of the Lord will be saved. But, how shall they ask Him to save them unless they believe in Him. And how can they believe in Him if they never heard about Him? And how can they hear about Him unless someone tells them?*

***2 Timothy 2:26 TLB** Then they will come to their senses and escape from Satan's trap of slavery to sin which he uses to catch them whenever he likes, and then they can begin doing the will of God.*

***Matthew 11:28** Come to Me all you that labor and are heavy laden, and I will give you rest.*

***James 4:7** Submit yourselves, therefore, to God. Resist the devil and he will flee from you.*

***Revelation 3:20** Behold, I stand at the door and knock. If any man hear My voice, and open the door, I will come in to him and will sup with Him and he with Me.*

1 Thessalonians 5:17 Pray without ceasing.

John 4:23 But the hour comes and now is when the true worshippers shall worship the Father in spirit and in truth: for the Father seeks such to worship Him.

Matthew 11:29 Take my yoke upon you and learn from Me: for I am meek and lowly in heart and you shall find rest for your souls.

Faith is a marathon, not a sprint.

Matthew 10: 22 And you shall be hated of all men for My name's sake: but he that endures to the end shall be saved.

We are saved for good works (Ephesians 2:10), not by good works. (Isaiah 64:6)

Ephesians 2:10 For we are His workmanship, created in Christ Jesus unto good works, which God has before ordained that we should walk in them.

Isaiah 64:6 But we are all as an unclean thing, and all our righteousness are as filthy rags; and we all do fade as a leaf; and our iniquities like the wind, have taken us away.

Tithing (money and/or time) is an indication of faith.

II Corinthians 9: 8-9 TLB God is able to make it up to you by giving you everything you need and more, so that there will not only be enough for your needs but plenty left over to give joyfully to others.

Matthew 6: 21 For where your treasure is, there will your heart be also.

***Psalms 37:4** Delight yourself also in the Lord; and He shall give you the desires of your heart.*

A lady holiday shopping is frustrated by not finding a parking spot. In desperation she prays, "Lord, if you will find me a parking spot, I'll attend church every Sunday for two months". As she turns the corner and heads down the next row, a parking spot shows up immediately. Without hesitation, she prays (1 Peter 5:7), "Lord never mind, I just found one!"

Answered prayer is never a coincidence (John 4:50-53). Initially, coincidence all too often gets the credit for answered prayer, but eventually one realizes there cannot be that many coincidences.

***1 Peter 5:7** Casting all your care on Him for He cares for you.*

***John 4:50-53** Jesus said unto him, "Go your way. Your son lives." And the man believed the word Jesus had spoken to him, and he went his way. And as he was now going down, his servants met him and told him, "Your son lives. Then he inquired of them the hour when he began to amend. And they said to him, "Yesterday at the seventh hour the fever left him." So the father knew that it was the same hour, in which Jesus said unto him, "Your son lives." And he believed and his whole house.*

Knowledge without understanding is rendered useless. Faith is the substitute for understanding (Matthew 26:2, 52-54, 74, Acts 8:29-31). Often faith is the answer to, "Why?" Believing there is a God is knowledge. (James 2:19) Believing in/on God is faith. (Ephesians 3:19, Acts 16:31) If all who did not understand everything Jesus said turned away, no one would be left.

Understanding can let you down because it may not always be there for you. Because you control faith, it can always be there. Peter may not have understood everything, but he had faith in what he did understand. (John 9:25, John 6:60, 66-69) It's not what we don't understand, spiritually, but what we do understand that convicts or comforts us.

__Matthew 26:2, 52-54, 74 TLB__ Jesus said to His disciples, "As you know the Passover celebration begins in two days, and I will be betrayed and crucified." "Put away your sword. All they that take the sword shall perish with the sword. Don't you realize that I could ask my Father for thousands of angels to protect us, and He would send them instantly. But if I did, how would the scriptures be fulfilled that describe what is happening now?" Then began Peter to curse and to swear saying, "I know not the man." And immediately the cock crowed.

__Acts 8:29-31 TLB__ The Holy Spirit said to Philip, "Go over and walk along beside the chariot." Philip ran over and heard what he was reading and asked, "Do you understand it?" "Of course not!" the Ethiopian eunuch replied. "How can I when there is no one to instruct me?" And he begged Philip to come up into the chariot and sit with him.

__James 2:19__ You believe there is one God; you do well: the devils also believe and tremble

__Ephesians 3:19__ And to know the love of Christ, which passes knowledge, that you might be filled with the fullness of God.

__Acts 16:31__ And they said believe on the Lord Jesus Christ and you shall be saved and your house.

__John 9:25__ He answered and said, "Whether He is a sinner or not, I know not: one thing I know that, whereas I was blind, now I see.

__John 6:60, 66-69 TLB__ Even His disciples said, "This is very hard to understand. Who can tell what He means?" At this point many of His disciples turned away and deserted Him. Then Jesus turned to the twelve and asked, "Are you going to?" Simon Peter replied, "Master, to whom shall we go? You have the words of eternal life. And we believe them and know you are the Christ, the Son of the living God."

Amazement beyond understanding: Jesus will reach down with His nail-scarred hands into the world's filth to retrieve a sinking stinking soul, and cleanse it with grace just because that unworthy person asked Him.

__Romans 5:8__ But God showed His great love for us by sending Christ to die for us while we were yet sinners.

__Psalms 8:4__ What is man that thou art mindful of him? And the son of man that thou look after him?

Physically, seeing is believing, but, spiritually, believing is seeing.

__Matthew 13:14__ And in them is fulfilled the prophesy of Isaiah, which says, "By hearing you will hear, and shall not understand; and seeing you shall see, and not perceive."

__John 9:39__ Then Jesus told him, "I have come into the world to give sight to those who are spiritually blind and to show those who think they see that they are blind."

__2 Corinthians 5:7__ For we walk by faith, not by sight.

Faith does not live by explanation, but by promises.

__John 14:2-3__ In My Father's house are many mansions: if it were not so I would have told you. I go to prepare a place for you. And *if I go and prepare a place for you, I will come again and receive you unto myself: that where I am there you may be also.*

2 Corinthians 5:7 For we walk by faith, not by sight.

Romans 1:17 For therein is the righteousness of God revealed from faith to faith, as it is written: the just shall live by faith.

Who is wiser in spiritual wisdom about Jesus, you or the devil and his demons? They know who God is, know their fate, obey Him, and tremble? (Matthew 8: 28-32) Faith trumps knowledge. Big difference between believing "there is a God (James 2:19) and believing on/in God. (Acts 16:31)

Matthew 8:28-32 And when He was come to the other side of the country of the Gadarenes, there he was met by two possessed with devils, coming out of the tombs and were so dangerous that no one could go through that area. And behold they screamed, "What do you want with us, Jesus? Have You come now to torment us before the time?" (Note: Notice they didn't want Jesus to torment them, but it was OK for them to torment these helpless men for who knows how long. Does this give you some idea of Satan's love and how he plays you?)

James 2:19 You believe there is one God; you do well: the devils also believe and tremble.

Acts 16:31 And they said believe on the Lord Jesus Christ and you shall be saved and your house.

Faith should be a blessing, not a burden.

2 Timothy 1:12 TLB That is why I am suffering here in jail, and I am certainly not ashamed of it, for I know the One in whom I trust, and am sure that He is able to safely guard all that I have given Him until the day of His return.

Faith is experiencing the peace deep within when trials exist on the surface. (John 14:1) Worry cannot go deeper within us than where it meets faith. (Philippians 4:6-7)

John 14:1 Let not your heart be troubled, you believe in God, believe also in Me.

Philippines 4:6-7 TLB Don't worry about anything; instead, pray about everything: tell God your needs and don't forget to thank Him for His answers. If you do this, you will experience God's peace which is far more wonderful than the human mind can understand. His peace will keep your thoughts and your hearts quiet and at rest as you trust in Christ Jesus.

Failure does not have to be fatal.

Matthew 26:74-75 Then began he to curse and to swear saying, "I don't even know the man!" And immediately the cock crowed. And Peter remembering the word of Jesus which said unto him, "Before the cock crows, you will deny me three times." And he went out and wept bitterly.

John 21:17 TLB Once more He asked him, "(Peter) Simon, son of John, are you even My friend?" Peter was grieved at the way Jesus asked the question this third time. "Lord, you know my heart. You know I am, he said. Jesus said, "Then feed my sheep."

A merciful attitude toward the spiritually needy is far better than the mere formality of religious duties.

__Matthew 9: 13__ But go and learn what that means, "I will have mercy and not sacrifice: for I am not come to call the righteous, but sinners to repentance."

God's plan was not for man to suffer (1 Corinthians 15:21-22). The first two chapters of Genesis before man sinned and the last chapter of Revelation after Satan has been cast into the lake of fire show the death-free, pain-free, tear-free, sin-free love between God/man. All of the Bibical chapters in between show God/sin/man. **Sin** (Isaiah 59:2, Romans 6:23, Romans 14:23) **causes suffering and death not God** (Matthew 9: 36-37, but because of sin, omnipotent God can use suffering to our good within His will (Matthew 27:50) as He teaches us. If sin did not exist, there would be no need to prepare for trials.

__1 Corinthians 15:21-22 TLB__ Death came into the world because of what one man (Adam) did, and it is because of what this other man (Christ) has done that now there is the resurrection from the dead. Everyone dies because all of us are related to Adam, being members of his sinful race, and wherever there is sin, death results. But all who are related to Christ shall rise again.

__Isaiah 59:2 TLB__ But there is a problem; your sins have cut you off from God. Because of your sin, He has turned away and will not listen anymore.

__Romans 6:23__ For the wages of sin is death, but the gift of God is eternal life through Jesus Christ our Lord.

__Romans 14:23__ But anyone who believes that something is wrong shouldn't do it. He sins if he does, for he thinks it is wrong, and so for him it is wrong. Anything that is done apart from what he feels is right is sin.

Matthew 9:36-37 TLB And what pity He felt for the crowds that came, because their problems were so great, and they didn't know what to do or where to go for help. They were like sheep without a shepherd.

Matthew 27:50 Then Jesus shouted out again, dismissed His spirit, and died.

Heaven was made for mankind. (John14:2) Hell was not. (Revelation 20:15) Hell is a Godless place for those who choose not to receive God's love and forgiveness. When you live on earth among God's people, you share some of their blessings (Matthew 5:45); not so in hell. Why would the God you rejected, prepare a place for you. You are on your own; isn't that what you wanted?

John 14:2 In My Father's house are many mansions. If it were not so, I would have told you. I go to prepare a place for you.

Revelation 20:15 And whosoever was not found written in the book of life was cast into the lake of fire.

Matthew 5:45 That you may be the children of your Father which is in heaven: for He makes the sun to shine on the evil and on the good, and sends rain on the just and on the unjust.

Giving and *helping* are often as opposite as *enabling* and *converting*. Be careful how and what you give.

Matthew 10:13-14 TLB And if it turns out to be a godly home, give it your blessing; if not, keep the blessing. Any city or home that does not welcome you; shake off the dust of that place from your feet as you leave.

Matthew 12:38-39 *Then certain of the scribes and of the Pharisees answered saying, "Master, we would see a sign from you." But, He answered and said unto them, "An evil and adulterous generation seeks after a sign; and there shall no sign be given to it, but the sign of the prophet, Jonah.*

Poverty does not eliminate giving.

Mark 12:42-44 *And there came a certain poor widow, and she threw in two pennies. And He called unto Him His disciples and said unto them, "Verily I say unto you, that this poor widow has cast more in than all they which have cast into the treasury."*

When it comes to Christ-like giving, some people will stop at nothing!

Matthew 25:45 *Then shall He answer them saying, "Verily I say unto you, "Inasmuch as you did it not to one of the least of these, you did it not to me."*

Not accepting God's forgiving love causes needless pain even unto death. Guilt without grace; sin without a Savior

Matthew 27:4-5 TLB *"I have sinned," Judas declared, "for I have betrayed an innocent man." "That's your problem," they retorted. Then he threw the money onto the floor of the Temple and went out and hanged himself.*

Romans 3:24 TLB *Yet now God declares us "not guilty" of offending Him, if we trust in Jesus Christ, who in His kindness freely takes away our sins.*

***1 Corinthians 15:3** I passed onto you right from the first what had been told to me, that Christ died for our sins just as the Scriptures said he would.*

God's love is often mistaken to be God's weakness. To save others He did not save Himself and come down off the cross.

***Revelation 1:8** "I am the alpha and the Omega, the beginning and the ending," says the Lord, "which is, and which was, and which is to come, the Almighty."*

***2 Peter 3:9** The Lord is not slack concerning His promise, as some men count slackness; but is longsuffering toward us, not willing that any should perish, but that all should come to repentance.*

***Matthew 27:42** He saved others; himself He cannot save. If He is the King of Israel, let Him now come down from the cross, and we will believe Him.*

Stress is the distance between our strength and God's strength.

***2 Corinthians 12:9** And He said unto me, "My grace is sufficient for you: for My strength is made perfect in weakness. Most gladly, therefore, will I rather glory in my infirmities, that the power of Christ may rest upon me.*

Must an unfaithful child who rejects the proper direction of a loving parent suffer the consequences? Has the child of loving parents ever been given the death penalty?

***Luke 15:11-16 TLB** A certain man had two sons: and the younger of them said to his father, "Father, I want my share of your estate now, instead of waiting until you die." His father agreed to divide his wealth between his two sons. A few days later this* *younger son packed all his belongings and took a trip to a distant land, and there wasted all his money on parties and prostitutes. About the time all his money was gone a great famine swept over the land, and he began to starve. He persuaded a local farmer to hire him to feed his pigs. The boy became so hungry that even the pods he was feeding the pigs looked good to him. And no one gave him anything.*

Luke 13:34-35 TLB O Jerusalem, Jerusalem! The city that murders the prophets. The city that stones those sent to help her. How often I have wanted to gather your children together even as a hen gathers protects her brood under her wings, but you wouldn't let me. And now your house is left desolate. And you will never again see Me until you say, "Welcome to Him who comes in the name of the Lord."

Do the best you can with what you've got, where you can, every chance you can.

Matthew 22:37 Jesus said unto him, "Thou shall love the Lord your God with all your heart, and with all your soul, and with all your mind."

God will not be a stand-in for your mind-made god.

Exodus 20:3 Thou shall have no other gods before Me.

Deuteronomy 7:9-10 TLB Understand, therefore, that the Lord your God is indeed God. He is the faithful God who keeps His covenant for a thousand generations and constantly loves those who love Him and obey His commands. But He does not hesitate to punish and destroy those who hate Him.

Know who God is; don't expect your mind-made god to get you to your mind-made heaven.

__Matthew 15:8-9 (Isaiah 29:13) TLB__ These people say they honor Me, but their hearts are far away. Their worship is worthless, for they teach their man-made laws instead of those from God.

__John 14:6__ Jesus said unto him, "I am the way, the truth, and the life: no man comes to the Father but by Me.

__Isaiah 45:22 TLB__ Let all the world look to Me for salvation! For I am God; there is no other.

__Luke 16:15__ And He said to them, "You are they which justify yourselves before man; but God knows your hearts: for that which is highly esteemed among men is abomination in the sight of God."

If one does not receive God for whom He is, then one cannot receive what God gives.

__Isaiah 44:6-8__ This is the Lord, Israel's King and Redeemer, the Lord Almighty, says "I am the First and the Last; there is no other God. Who else can tell you what is going to happen in the days ahead? Let them tell you if they can and thus prove their power. Let them do as I have done since ancient time. Do not tremble; do not be afraid. Have I not proclaimed from ages past what my purposes are for you? You are my witnesses – is there any other God? No! There is no other Rock – no not one!"

__James 1:12__ Blessed is the man that endures temptation: for when he is tried, he shall receive the crown of life, which the Lord has promised to those that love Him.

1 Peter 5:4 And when the chief Shepherd shall appear; you shall receive a crown of glory that fades not away.

There is a difference between boldness and pride.

Hebrews 4:16 Let us, therefore, come boldly unto the throne of grace, that we may obtain mercy, and find grace to help in time of need.

Proverbs 16:18 Pride goes before destruction, and an arrogant spirit before a fall.

Galatians 6:14 But God forbid that I should glory, save in the cross of the Lord Jesus Christ, by whom my interest in the world's attractive things was killed long ago, and the world's interest in me is also long dead.

Sin cannot be ignored. You can temporarily delay, but, eventually you must deal with the consequences of sin. What sin can do to you - death. What you can do to sin - repent. Sincere repentance is always followed by joy.

Galatians 6:7 Be not deceived; God is not mocked; whatsoever a man sows, that shall he also reap.

James 1:15 Then when lust has conceived, it brings forth sin; and sin, when it is finished, brings forth death.

Romans 6:16 TLB Don't you realize you can choose your own master? You can choose sin (with death) or else obedience (with acquittal). The one to whom you offer yourselves – he will take you and be your master and you will be his slave.

Romans 6:23 For the wages of sin is death, but the gift of God is eternal life through Jesus Christ our Lord.

John 1:12 But as many as received Him, to them gave He power to become the sons of God even to them that believe on His name.

If sin is no big deal, then why did Judas commit suicide; Peter weep; the thief on the cross ask Jesus to remember him? And you; what about you?

Matthew 27:4-5 TLB "I have sinned," Judas declared, "For I have betrayed an innocent man." "That's your problem," they retorted. Then Judas threw the money onto the floor of the Temple and went out and hanged himself.

Matthew 26:75 And Peter remembered the word of Jesus which said to him, "Before the cock crow, you shall deny me three times, and he went out and wept bitterly.

Luke 23:40-42 TLB But the other criminal protested, "Don't you even fear God when you are dying? We deserve to die for our evil deeds, but this man hasn't done one thing wrong." Then he said, "Jesus, remember me when You come into Your Kingdom."

Sin is never free. The blood of Jesus cleanses us from all sin, but not excuses for not following Him. When Calvary is rejected, there is no other cure for sin.

1 Peter 2:24 Who His own self bare our sins in His own body, on a tree, that we, being dead to sins, should live unto righteousness: by whose stripes we are healed.

1 John 1:7 But if we walk in the light as He is in the light, we have fellowship one

with another, and the blood of Jesus Christ His Son cleanses us from all sin.

All decisions, *especially* spiritual, have consequences.

Joshua 24:15 _And if it seem evil for you to serve the Lord, choose you this day whom you will serve; whether the gods your ancestors served beyond the Euphrates? Or will it be the gods of the Amorites in whose land you now live? But as for me and my family, we will serve the Lord._

Matthew 10:33 _But whosoever shall deny Me before men, him shall I deny before My Father which is in heaven._

Last August I received a letter from the county treasurer stating the amount of my property taxes and a deadline of September 30th for paying them. This caused me to think about paying my taxes. Do I really want to pay them or not? I could have a lot of fun with that money. I thought and thought about paying even to the point of waking up in the night debating in my mind (John 3:18). I didn't start to put anything away in case I decided to pay, and it really didn't matter as the county treasurer never seemed to mind. In fact, I wondered if maybe this decision would just go away on its own, if I just kept procrastinating.

September 30th was just a couple days away, and I had heard nothing more from the treasurer. Things were going well. Recently, I had not lost any sleep over the decision to pay the taxes or not. Although I had spent money on frivolous toys, I really had not decided not to pay the taxes; I just had not decided.

In October, I got a notice that my taxes had not been paid. I was surprised because I figured since I had not heard from them for a few weeks, they had probably forgotten about me. I called politely explaining that I didn't mean to offend anyone at the treasurer's office, but I just hadn't decided whether to pay or not. It isn't like I won't, I just hadn't decided yet. They seemed like caring people, and offered to help me in any way they could. I took that as a sign that anyone that nice would never hurt me. Getting by with no penalty so far encouraged me to just delay the decision longer.

As time went by, and I kept explaining that I just hadn't made a decision, I received a notice that my property would be for sale at a public auction. Again, I explained that I had not made a decision on whether I would pay my taxes or not. They stated that no decision was a decision. (John 3:18)

After the proceeds from my property sale were used to pay my taxes, I decided I would pay my taxes. (Romans 14:11-12) Unfortunately, I realized that although I can delay the decision, eventually there comes a judgment day when no decision is a decision (Matthew 12:36), and I was too late to save my belongings (Luke 9:24).

__John 3:18__ He that believes on Him is not condemned: but he that believeth not is condemned already, because he has not believed in the name of the only begotten Son of God.

__Romans 14:11-12__ "For it is written, as I live," says the Lord, "Every knee shall bow to me, and every tongue shall confess to God."

__Matthew 12:36__ But I say unto you, that every idle word that men shall speak, they shall give an account therefore in the day of judgment.

__Luke 9:24__ For whosoever shall save his life shall lose it: but whosoever will lose his life for my sake, the same shall save it.

After a bath and dressed in his Sunday best clothes, a young farm boy runs out the front door, through the yard, over the gate, and begins chasing the pigs in the mud, manure, and stink of the pig pen.

Not realizing that when you play with pigs, you'll get some stink on you, he falls into the mire covering himself with smelly mud and skinning his knee.

Crying as he climbs over the gate, he runs toward the house. His mother, who keeps the house spotless, sees him coming. She stops him outside the front door. He wants in. She says, "No way."

His mother leads him to the garden hose and washes him off (Acts 22:16). She then takes him in her arms into the house to dry him, wipe away his tears, put a band aid on his scratched knee and feed him (Revelation 7:17).

It wasn't her child that mom didn't love when she wouldn't initially let him into the house, it was the mud (John 3:16). No matter how dirty her son got, there was always plenty of water to clean him. Once he was clean, he was welcome into her home. (Romans 5:20, Matthew 25:34) No matter how great or how many sins (mud) cover us, there is always enough water (grace) (Romans 3:24) to cleanse us by a loving, forgiving God.

Acts 22:16 TLB And now, why delay? Go and be baptized, and be cleansed from your sins, calling on the name of the Lord.

Revelation 7:17 For the Lamb which is in the midst of the throne shall feed them, and shall lead them unto living fountains of waters: and God shall wipe away all tears from their eyes.

John 3:16 For God so loved the world that He gave His only begotten Son that whosoever believes on Him shall not perish but have everlasting life.

Romans 5:20 Moreover the law entered, that the offense might abound. But where sin abounded, grace did much more abound!!

Matthew 25:34 Then shall the King say unto them on His right hand, "Come you blessed of My Father, inherit the kingdom prepared for you from the foundation of the world.

Romans 3:24 TLB Yet now God declares us "not guilty" of offending Him, if we trust in Jesus Christ, who in His kindness freely takes away our sins.

Justice = get what you deserve. Mercy = get what you don't deserve. (James 2:13) Grace = get much more than you deserve, unmerited favor. (Romans 5:20) Spiritually, *never* ask God for justice (Romans 6:23, 1 Peter 4:18). One cries for justice until mercy is needed.

James 2:13 TLB For there will be no mercy to those who have shown no mercy. But if you have been merciful, then God's mercy toward you will win out over His judgment against you.

Romans 5:20 TLB The Ten Commandments were given so that all could see the extent of their failure to obey God's laws. But the more we see our sinfulness, the more we see God's abounding grace forgiving us.

Romans 6:23 For the wages of sin is death, but the gift of God is eternal life through Jesus Christ our lord.

1 Peter 4:18 And if the righteous scarcely be saved, where will the ungodly and the sinner appear.

There are no atheists in heaven or hell; only on this earth.

Romans 14:10-12 But why do you judge your brother? Or why do you look down on him? For we shall all stand before the judgment seat of Christ. For it is written, "As I live," says the Lord, "every knee shall bow to Me, and every tongue shall confess to God. So then, every one of us shall give an account of himself to God.

Psalms 53:1 TLB Only fools say in their hearts, "There is no God." They are corrupt and their actions are evil; no one does good.

There is as much difference between "want" and "do" as there is between "can't" and "won't."

Romans 7:18 For I know that in me (that is in my flesh) dwells no good thing: for to will is present with me: but how to perform that which is good I find not.

Difference between *Law* and *Love*

Young girl at a party was asked to do sinful acts. She said, "No." When asked, "Are you afraid your dad will hurt you?" She replied, "No, I'm afraid I'll hurt my dad."

Romans 8:5 TLB Those that let themselves be controlled by their lower nature live only to please themselves, but those who follow after the Holy Spirit find themselves doing those things that please God.

As we all have proven, there *is pleasure in sin*, but only for a season. Inevitably, sorrow follows sin.

Hebrews 11:24-26 TLB It was by faith Moses, when he grew up, refused to be treated as the grandson of the king, but chose to share ill-treatment with God's people instead of enjoying the fleeting pleasures of sin. He thought it was better to suffer for the promised Christ than to own all the treasures of Egypt, for he was looking forward to the great reward that God would give him.

__Proverbs 14:13__ Laughter can conceal a heavy heart; when the laughter ends, the grief remains.

__Luke 15:11-16 TLB__ A certain man had two sons: and the younger of them said to his father, "Father, I want my share of your estate now, instead of waiting until you die." His father agreed to divide his wealth between his two sons. A few days later this younger son packed all his belongings and took a trip to a distant land, and there wasted all his money on parties and prostitutes. About the time all his money was gone a great famine swept over the land, and he began to starve. He persuaded a local farmer to hire him to feed his pigs. The boy became so hungry that even the pods he was feeding the pigs looked good to him. And no one gave him anything.

__Matthew 13:40-42__ As therefore the tares are gathered and burned in the fire; so shall it be in the end of the world. The Son of man shall send forth His angles, and they shall gather out of His kingdom all things that offend, and them which do iniquity; and shall cast them into a furnace of fire: there will be wailing and gnashing of teeth.

Many habitually thirsty people prefer a sip of water rather than enjoy the refreshing life-giving flowing well that's offered.

__John 4:14__ But whosoever drinks of the water that I shall give him shall never thirst: but the water I shall give him shall be in him a well of water springing up into everlasting life.

__John 7:37-38 TLB__ On the last day, the climax of the holidays, Jesus shouted to the crowds, "If anyone is thirsty, let him come to Me and drink. For the Scriptures declare that rivers of living water shall flow from the innermost being of anyone who believes in Me.

Revelation 7:17 *For the Lamb which is in the midst of the throne shall feed them, and shall lead them into living fountains of waters; and God shall wipe away all tears from their eyes.*

Like undisciplined children, those who have not accepted Jesus as Savior do what they want (Romans 6:20-21, Romans 8:5) seeking satisfaction. They have created a lifestyle they want, not what they need.

Christians do what needs to be done (Romans 6: 16-18, 22) receiving joy. If you are filled with joy (John 15:11), there is no room for anything else. Oil and water are more compatible than joy/sadness, or peace/doubt. Love and peace blend with joy.

Romans 6:20-21 *For when you were servants of sin, you were free from righteousness. And what was the result? Evidently not good since you are ashamed now even to think about those things you used to do. For, in all of them the end is death.*

Romans 8:5 *For they that are after the flesh do mind the things of the flesh; but they that are after the Spirit the things of the spirit.*

Romans 6:16-18, 22 *Know you not that to whom you yield yourselves servants to obey, his servants you are to whom you obey: whether of sin unto death, or of obedience unto righteousness. But God be thanked, that you were the servants of sin, but you have obeyed from the heart that form of doctrine which was delivered you. Being then made free from sin, you become the servants of righteousness.*

John 15:11 *These things have I spoken to you that My joy might remain in you and that your joy might be full.*

There is a difference between passion (Acts 4:18-20) and caffeine. (Matthew 23:5-6) Inward devotion trumps outward emotion every time. (John 2:23-25)

Acts 4:18-20 So the Jewish council called Peter and John back in and told them never again to speak about Jesus. But Peter and John replied, "You decide whether God wants us to obey you instead of Him?! We cannot stop telling about the wonderful things we saw Jesus do and heard Him say!"

Matthew 23:5-6 TLB Everything the scribes and Pharisees do is done for show. They act holy by wearing on their arms large prayer boxes with Scripture verses inside, and by lengthening the memorial fringe on their robes. And, how they love to sit at the head table at banquets, and in the reserved pews in the synagogue.

Matthew 13:5-6 And some fell on stony places where they had not much earth: and at once they sprung up: because they had no deepness of earth and when the sun was up, they were scorched; and because they had no root, they withered away.

John 2:23-25 TLB Because of the miracles He did in Jerusalem at the Passover celebration, many people were convinced that He was indeed the Messiah. But Jesus didn't trust them, for He knew mankind to the core. No one needed to tell Him how changeable human nature is!

Many want to serve God – as a consultant!

Romans 11:34 For who has known the mind of the Lord? Who knows enough to be His counselor and guide?

No law can make you moral. (Romans 3:20-22) You cannot legislate God's morality. (Ephesians 2:8) The law is to identify immorality. (Romans 2:12-15, Romans 5:20)

Romans 3:20-22 TLB Now do you see it? No one can ever be made right in God's sight by doing what the law commands. For the more we know of God's laws, the clearer it becomes that we aren't obeying them; His laws serve only to make us see that we are sinners. But God has now shown us a different way to heaven – not by "being good enough," and trying to keep His laws, but by a new way (though not new, really, for the Old Testament told about it long ago). Now God says He will accept and acquit us, declare us "not guilty," if we trust Jesus Christ to take away our sins. And we all can be saved in the same way, by coming to Christ no matter who we are or what we have been like.

Ephesians 2:8 For by grace are you saved through faith; and that not of yourselves, it is the gift of God.

Romans 2:12-15 God will punish sin wherever it is found. He will punish the heathen when they sin, even though they never had God's written laws, for down in their hearts they know right from wrong. God's laws are written within them: their own conscience accuses them, or sometimes excuses them. And God will punish the Jews for sinning because they have His written laws, but don't obey them. They know what is right, but don't do it. After all, Salvation is not given to those who know what to do, unless they do it.

Romans 5:20 The Ten Commandments were given so that all could see the extent of their failure to obey God's laws. But the more we see our sinfulness, the more we see God's abounding grace forgiving us.

"Stinkin thinkin"

1 John 1:10 If we say we have not sinned, we make Him a liar, and His word is not in us.

God does not dwell on all the reasons we give Him for not loving us. (Romans 5:8) Rather, He sees all the potential we have with His help. (1 John 3:1, Philippians 4:13)

Romans 5:8 But God commended His love toward us, in that, while we were yet sinners, Christ died for us.

1 John 3:1 Behold, what manner of love the Father has bestowed upon us, that we should be called the sons of God: therefore the world knows us not, because it knew Him not.

Philippians 4:13 I can do all things through Christ which strengthens me.

Success is not the goal. Succeeding at sin is failure.

Matthew 26:14-15 TLB Then Judas Iscariot, one of the twelve apostles, went to the chief priests and asked, "How much will you pay me to get Jesus into your hands?" And they gave him thirty pieces silver coins.

Mark 8:36 And what shall it profit a man if he shall gain the whole world, and lose his soul?

Philippians 3:8 TLB Yes, everything else is worthless when compared with the priceless gain of knowing Christ Jesus, my Lord. I have put aside all else, counting it as worth less than nothing in order that I can have Christ.

Reputation vs. Character: Reputation is whom people think you are. (Matthew 27: 39-40) Character is whom you are. (John 14:6, 1 Peter 2:24)

Matthew 27:39-40 TLB And the people passing by hurled abuse shaking their heads at Him and saying, "So, You can destroy the Temple and build it again in three days, can You? Well, then come down from the cross, if You are the Son of God!"

John 14:6 Jesus said unto them, "I am the way, the truth, and the life; no man comes unto the Father, but by Me.

1 Peter 2:24 Who by his own self bare our sins in His own body on the tree, that we, being dead to sins, should live unto righteousness: by whose stripes we are healed.

There is a difference between heart burn (Luke 21:26-27) and a burning heart. (Philippines 1:21, Luke 6:45, 24:32, Revelation 3:15-16)

Luke 21:26-27 Men's hearts failing them for fear, and for looking after these things which are coming on the earth: for the powers of heaven shall be shaken.

Philippines 1:21 For to me to live is Christ, and to die is gain.

Luke 6:45 A good man out of the good treasures of his heart brings forth that which is good. And an evil man out of the evil treasures of his heart brings forth that which is evil: for of the abundance of the heart his mouth speaks.

Luke 24:32 And they said one to another, "did not our heart burn within us while He talked with us by the way, and while He opened to us the scriptures?

Revelation 3:15-16 TLB *I know you well – you are neither hot nor cold; I wish you were one or the other! But since you are merely lukewarm, I will spit you out of My mouth!*

My doctor, Dr. Chris, is a great physician and friend. He was my delivery-room doctor (Isaiah 49:1) when I was born. As a child I went to him for colds, preventative shots, prescriptions, etc. (Mark 10:14-16)

When I was older, he repaired my broken wrist, medicated my acne, and treated my mononucleosis. Later, when I was diagnosed with breast cancer, he over saw the various treatments from several specialists. His bed-side manner is so loving, (Psalms 36:7) and compassionate. (Mark 1:41-42)

It was no wonder that one day at work I bragged (Psalms 118:21) about Dr. Chris when someone else mentioned his name. Much to my surprise another co-worker started on a tirade about my doctor. After letting him ventilate, I asked why he was so opposed to my friend and doctor?

He stated that Dr. Chris was his delivery-room doctor as well. However, since that time the doctor had done nothing to benefit his well-being. (Ephesians 1:4) He agreed with me that this doctor had many skills concerning medicine, diseases, broken bones, etc, but he had not used any of these skills on him.

Surprisingly, I asked what ailments for which he had gone to this doctor. I went from surprised to shocked when he told me he had not seen the doctor since the day he was born. The obvious question was, "How can you blame this physician if you had never gotten an appointment to see him?"

"Why would I go to him? Obviously, he knows I exist since he is the one who delivered me, so he should call me (Revelation 3:20). "Do you always answer the door when someone knocks?" was my reply? Doesn't he know sometime in my life I would need a doctor? (Matthew 9:11-13) Yes, he did call my mother a few days after my birth, but she never returned the call. I've seen him at various places, but I always avoided him.

We use home remedies and the emergency room as needed, but we would never go to someone who cares so little for his patients. (John 10:14) On forms that ask who my doctor is, I write his name, (1 John 2:4) but we don't need a doctor. When I twisted my back and was off work for a few days, he never called. And, now this lump on my neck, and he doesn't care. He has money, all this medical expertise, and he doesn't even care enough to call. That's your wonderful doctor!

I asked him if he wanted me to schedule an appointment for him with Dr. Chris. He adamantly stated, "No! Why would I want to see him as he doesn't want anything to do with me since I am not a his patient. He is a worthless doctor."

My reply was, "I understand why Dr. Chris is worthless to someone who doesn't doctor with him, but to me he has not only saved my life, but enhanced it too. (1 Peter 3:12) I will continue to praise his accomplishments in my life and use him."

Although the timing didn't seem appropriate to ask, yet, I wondered, "What responsibility has my co-worker accepted? Worthless physician or worthless patient? Why blame a physician he refuses to see?" (Isaiah 59:2)

Isaiah 49:1 Listen, O isles, unto me; and hearken, you people, from far; the Lord has called me from the womb, from the bowels of my mother has He made mention of my name.

Mark 10:14-16 But when Jesus saw it He was much displeased, and said to them, "Suffer the little children to come to me, and forbid them not; for such is the kingdom of heaven. Verily, I say to you, whosoever shall not receive the kingdom of God as a little child, he shall not enter therein." And He took them up in His arms, put His hands on them, and blessed them.

Psalms 36:7 TLB How precious is Your unfailing love, O, God! All humanity finds shelter in the shadow of Your wings.

Mark 1:41-42 And Jesus moved with compassion, put forth His hand and touched him, and said unto him, "I want to." And as soon as He had spoken, immediately, the leprosy departed from him, and he was cleansed.

Psalms 18:21 For I have kept the ways of the Lord; and have not wickedly departed from my God.

Ephesians 1:4 According as He has chosen us in Him before the foundation of the world, that we should be holy and without blame before Him in love.

Revelation 3:20 Behold, I stand at the door and knock. If any man hear My voice, and open the door, I will come in to him and will sup with Him and he with Me.

Matthew 9:11-13 TLB The Pharisees were indignant, "Why does your teacher associate with men like that?" "Because people who are well don't need a doctor; it's the sick people who do!" was Jesus' reply. Then He added, "Go away and learn the meaning of this verse of Scripture, 'It isn't your sacrifices and your gifts I care about – it's that you have some pity.' My job down here on earth is to get sinners back to God – not to worry about the good people."

John 10:14 I am the good shepherd, and know My sheep, and am known of them.

1 John 2:4 He that says, "I know Him," and keeps not His commandments, is a liar, and the truth is not in him."

1 Peter 3:12 For the eyes of the Lord are over the righteous; and His ears are open to their prayers. But the face of the Lord is against them that do evil.

Isaiah 59:2 But your iniquities have separated between you and your God, and your sins have hid His face from you, that He will not hear.

As I sit here in rehab, I remember the last time I was here. I met a counselor, Jess, who was very instrumental in my recovery.

One day Jess asked me if I would help him with an idea he had for assisting the needy. (Mark 16:15) I read his plan, decided it was a good one, and volunteered my assistance.

When Jess got me out of rehab, he gave me a list of people and organizations to meet and also the presentation reminding me that some people would be opposed to this new action. (Mark 13:13)

I, successfully, devoted my time and effort toward Jess's plan. Because Jess was always there to encourage me, (Matthew 28:20) even during the not-so-good days, we became devoted friends. If I had a problem, Jess was there. He was a comfort through my son's problems, an unbearable boss, mom's terminal cancer, even the rough spots in my marriage. When Jess's plan went viral, an announcement came that I had been selected as "Citizen of the Year."

As the honored guest of the dinner-party in two weeks, I was asked to submit a list of friends I wanted to attend. After much deliberation, I decided not to invite Jess. I just couldn't see a disheveled person like Jess at a black-tie party. Jess loved parties (John 2:1-2), but people just would not understand. This was my time to make some very influential friends, and I didn't want to miss the opportunity.

I tried to make myself believe Jess's attendance would make <u>them</u> uneasy when really it was <u>me</u> that would have been uncomfortable. In my opinion, this was not Jess's kind of party. Besides, this party was about me, and I didn't want to share the attention with Jess. Explaining his plan, which the party-goers really needed to hear, would reduce the time for my accolades.

At the party I had this lonely, hollow feeling (Psalms 107:8-9). Something was missing and no matter how many compliments I got, no matter how much I drank, no matter how many pats my back received, this feeling would not go away. I recognized the terminal feeling because it was the same one that initially sent me to rehab. Occasionally, when I overheard party-goers laughing or degrading Jess, I just smiled, asked "Who's Jess?", and walked away. (Matthew 26:72)

Now after a relapse and back in rehab, I admittedly realize Jess should have been the honored guest. The plan was his, the dirty work was his, the intestinal fortitude was his. He allowed me to share the success just to see me smile when he could have offered my part to someone else and left me in rehab. His plan was so perfect it would have succeeded no matter who helped.

Jess was a devoted friend when I needed help, but when it came time to celebrate and advance his accomplishments, I wasn't a friend. He came to my rescue and made me something I never could have been without him. Jess saw me not for whom I was, but for whom I could be, I walked away rather than admit I knew him. I wonder if Jess could ever forgive me. Would he help me again if I asked? (Matthew 18: 21-22, Matthew 26:74-75, John 21:14-15)

Then I realized Jess's healing plan was not for everyone else but me, but included me! Not thinking Jess would help me was not understanding Jess or his plan. (Matthew 18:21-22)

__Mark 16:15__ And He said to them, "Go ye into all the world and preach the gospel to every creature."

__Mark 13:13__ And you shall be hated of all men for my name's sake: but he that endures to the end, the same shall be saved.

__Matthew 28:20__ Teaching them to observe all things whatsoever I have commanded you: and, lo, I am with you always, even to the end of the world.

__John 2:1-2__ And the third day there was a marriage in Cana of Galilee; and the mother of Jesus was there. And both Jesus was called, and His disciples to the marriage.

__Psalms 107:8-9__ Oh that men would praise the Lord for His goodness, and for His wonderful works to the children of men. For He satisfies the longing soul, and fills the hungry soul with goodness.

__Matthew 26:72__ And, again he denied with an oath, "I do not know the man."

Matthew 18:21-22 *Then came Peter to Him and said, "Lord, how often shall my brother sin against me, and I forgive him? Till seven times?" Jesus said to him, "I say not to you, until seven times; but until seventy times seven."*

Matthew 26:74-75 *Then, began he to curse and to swear, saying, "I know not the man." And, immediately the cock crowed. And Peter remembered the word of Jesus, which said to him, "Before the cock crow, you shall deny Me thrice. And, he went out and wept bitterly.*

John 21:14-15 TLB *This was the third time Jesus had appeared to us since His return from the dead. After breakfast Jesus to Simon Peter, "Simon, son of John, do you love Me more than these?" "Yes," Simon replied, "you know I am your friend." "Then feed my lambs," Jesus told him.*

Matthew 18:21-22 *Then came Peter to Him and said, "Lord, how often shall my brother sin against me, and I forgive him? Till seven times?" Jesus said to him, "I say not to you, until seven times: but, until seventy times seven."*

The problem is not if God will forgive you (I John 1:9, Romans 8:1), but if you will forgive yourself. (Matthew 27:3-5)

1 John 1:9 *If we confess our sins, He is faithful and just to forgive us our sins and to cleanse us from all unrighteousness.*

Romans 8:1 *There is therefore now no condemnation to them which are in Christ Jesus, who walk not after the flesh, but after the Spirit.*

Matthew 27:3-5 *Then Judas, which had betrayed Him, when he saw that He was condemned, repented himself (not to Jesus), and brought again the thirty pieces of silver to the chief priests and elders saying, "I have sinned in that I have betrayed the innocent blood." And they said, "What is that to us? See you to that." And he cast down the pieces of silver in the temple, and departed, and went out and hanged himself.*

Life cannot be divided into secular and sacred, giving God only the sacred. God is Lord of all or not Lord at all (Matthew 6:24). Would you tell the world's greatest surgeon she can remove your splinters but nothing else and then condemn her for your bursted appendix? God will not settle for second place in your life (Matthew 16:24, Exodus 20:3).

Matthew 6:24 No man can serve two masters: for either he will hate the one and love the other; or else he will hold to the one and despise the other. You cannot serve God and mammon.

Matthew 16:24 Then Jesus said to His disciples, "If any man will come after Me, let him deny himself, and take up his cross, and follow Me.

Exodus 20:3 Thou shall have no other gods before me.

I called a loyal friend who works for a GPS company to chart my course on a bucket-list trip. She said she had heard of my destination but could not find any information in their memory bank. However, she knew someone who said not to worry just keep driving, and as long as I didn't break any traffic laws, I'd get there (Romans 3:20). Also, she told me that many, many people want to go to the same destination, and seem to think there are many ways to get there, with one just as good as the other. (Matthew 7:13-14, John 14:6)

I thought the GPS person would drive me to my destination, but they only give the directions. I'm responsible for following the directions. Maps and GPS's are wonderful, but they can't pick your destination, and you cannot tell them where you want to go if you have not decided. If your destination is heaven, be careful whom you ask for directions. (Matthew 24:11) Remember, you're the one who is choosing. Just because she has directions doesn't mean she has the right ones or knows how to use them. (John 14:6 found in God's GPS map). Choose your GPS guide well (Matthew 16:15-16).

Romans 3:20 TLB Now do you see it? No one can ever be made right in God's sight by doing what the law commands. For the more we know of God's laws the clearer it becomes that we are not obeying them. His laws serve only to make us see that we are sinners.

Matthew 7:13-14 Enter in at the straight gate: for wide is the gate and broad is the way that leads to destruction, and many there be who go that way. Because straight is the gate and narrow is the way, which leads to life, and few there be that find it.

John 14:6 Jesus said to them, "I am the way, the truth, and the life. No man comes to the father but by Me."

Matthew 24:11 And many false prophets shall rise, and deceive many.

Matthew 16:15-16 He said to them, "But whom say you that I am?" And Simon Peter answered and said, "Thou art the Christ, the Son of the living God."

LIFE

Several years ago, my family often drove by a house in our community that became known as our "dream house". A beautiful brick house with manicured lawn, shrubs, flowers, trees, big back yard with a waterfall, three-car garage, all we had dreamed.

One day as we drove by, we mustered enough courage to ask the owners if we could see the inside of "our dream house." To our amazement the interior was more beautiful than the outside. The owners had gotten the design from a well-known carpenter/architect and had done the work themselves. Reminiscing, they laughingly told about the arguments (Romans 5: 3-5), financial restrictions, nearly overwhelming obstacles (I Corinthians 10:13), joy (Galatians 5: 22), and the benefits of working together toward their goal. Now they were content, abundantly enjoying (John 10:10) their home despite occasionally giving it needed attention as all homes need.

Since they emphasized how essential their carpenter had been not only with the plan, but also with willing advice when their work hit a snag (I Peter 5:7), we contacted him about remodeling our house's interior. Although feasible, after counting the cost, do-it-yourself labor and time away from our leisurely activities, we decided it wasn't worth it. (Luke 14:27-28) We did, however, maintain the house's exterior as we tried to impress passersby (John 12:43).

Now years later as we drive by "our dream house," we regretfully laugh at our ill-fated decision. (Galatians 5:19) Remembering their smiling faces, I now realize the difference between joy (Galatians 5:22) and laughter (Ecclesiastes 7:6).

We tried to sell our house. Many people liked the exterior (Matthew 23:28), but when they saw the interior, they walked away (Luke 16:15). Warped floors from leaking pipes, frayed wiring, damaged drywall, a crumbling foundation are not good selling points.

When we begin to lament what living in our dream house would have been like, we convert to activities that numb our senses or replace our regretful thoughts. Regrets don't get easier with time; despite trying to numb them. Our house could have been a real asset to us in our old age instead of the liability it is now (II Timothy 2:15).

Romans 5:3-5 And not only so, but we glory in tribulations also; knowing that tribulation works patience; and patience, experience; and experience hope; and hope makes us not ashamed; because the love of God is shed abroad in our hearts by the Holy Ghost which is given to us.

1 Corinthians 10:13 But remember this - the wrong desires that come into your life aren't anything new and different. Many others have faced exactly the same problems before you. And no temptation is irresistible. You can trust God to keep the temptation from becoming so strong that you can't stand up against it, for He has promised this and will do what He says. He will show you how to escape temptation's power so that you can bear up patiently against it.

Galatians 5:22 But the fruit of the Spirit is love, joy, peace, kindness, goodness, and faithfulness.

John 10:10 The thief comes not but to steal, and to kill, and to destroy; I am come that you might have life and have it more abundantly.

1 Peter 5:7 Casting all your cares on Him for He cares for you.

Luke 14:27-28 And whosoever does not bear his cross, and come after Me, cannot be My disciple.

John 12:43 For they loved the praise of men more than the praise of God.

Galatians 5:19 TLB But when you follow your own wrong inclinations your lives will produce these evil results: impure thoughts, eagerness for lustful pleasure …

Ecclesiastes 7:6 TLB Indeed, a fool's laughter is quickly gone, like thorns crackling in a fire. This also is meaningless.

Matthew 23:28 Even so you outwardly appear righteous to men, but within you are full of hypocrisy and iniquity.

Luke 16:15 And He said to them, "You are they which justify yourselves before men; but God knows your hearts: for that which is highly esteemed among men is abomination in the sight of God.

2 Timothy 2:15 Study to show yourself approved to God, a workman that need not to be ashamed, knowing what His word says and means.

Each of us has the ability to be an accountant and is encouraged to be one.

Luke 14:28 For which of you, intending to build a tower sits not down first and counts the cost to know if he is sufficient to finish it.

Romans 14:12 So then every one of us shall give an account of himself to God.

For my Philosophy 101 Class I am to make a statement and then defend it as the class tries to discredit it. I decided to state that *"On June 6, 1944, the sun came up in the east just like it will tomorrow morning."* What an epiphany!

After presenting my statement, one classmate asked, "What are your credentials for making such a statement? Aren't you just an ordinary classmate (Matthew 13: 55-57) with no experience on solar systems? Of course, a step toward discrediting any statement is to discredit the person who made the statement.

My rebuttal was that I had studied history and found that on June 6th 1944, the sun, according to historians, had indeed come up in the east. That was challenged by asking if I believed everything I read in the history books or internet. My reply, "No, only when evidence proves the statement to be true. Don't take my word for truth; do your own research."

"How can you prove the sun came up on that day without a witness?" I said, "I have a witness." A WWII soldier who stormed Omaha Beach that day stood up. He was asked if the sun came up in the east on June 6, 1944. He stated that because it was cloudy and overcast, he did not see the sunrise under the circumstances. However, since he could see the beach, the sunlight had come through the eastern clouds which meant the sun had come up. This was an obvious opening for the class's argument. Since my witness did not actually see the sun come up in the east, it is possible that it did not rise in the east but from some other direction? In fact, several classmates admitted that they had never seen a sunrise from any direction. Just because the sun came up in the east in France, doesn't mean it would come up in the east in the United States and decades later.

Another classmate theorized that even if the sun has come up consistently in the east, it is no guarantee that it will rise in the east tomorrow. In fact, he states that tomorrow's sunrise will be in the north because the north is really the east. History has had it wrong. Until proven wrong he felt he is just as right as someone who believes the sun will rise in the east. I stated that the sun has absolutely always come up in the east. He stated that there are no absolutes. My thought was, "no absolutes? Isn't what you said an absolute?"

Finally the class asked me to admit I was wrong about the sun. If I would, they said they would tell everyone what a great debater I was (Matthew 4: 8-11).

Creating doubt, by trying to discredit history (Matthew 28: 12-15), a witness (John 9:24-25), truth (John 14:6, John 8:32), and me were the class's objectives (Hebrews 11:6). They became more enamored with possibilities than with facts.

When the class voted as to whether they believed *"the sun did rise in the east on June 6, 1944, and will rise in the east again tomorrow"*, some apathetic students admitted that doubt had entered their thinking while a few were undecided because it was irrelevant to them. However, because of their faith and experiences with the Son, others believed my statement (Mark 4:9).

***Matthew 13:55-57** Is not this the carpenter's son? Is not His mother, Mary; and His brothers, James, Jonas, Simon, and Judas? And His sisters; Are they not all with us? How can this man be so great? And they became angry with Him. But Jesus said to them, "A prophet is not without honor, except in his own country, and in his own house."*

***Matthew 4:8-11** Again, the devil took Him up into an exceeding high mountain, and showed Him all the kingdoms of the world, and the glory of them. And he said to Him, "All these things will I give You if You will fall down and worship me." Then said Jesus to him, "Get thee behind me Satan: for it is written Thou shall worship the Lord thy God and Him only shall you serve." Then the devil left Him, and behold angels came and ministered to Him.*

***Matthew 28:12-15** And when they were assembled with the elders, and had taken counsel, they gave large money to the* *soldiers. Saying, "Say His disciples came by night, and stole Him away while we slept. If the governor hears about it, the council promised, we will stand up for you and everything will be all right.*

John 9:24-25 Then again called they the man who had been blind and said to him, "Give God the praise. We know this man is a sinner." He answered and said, "Whether He be a sinner or not, I don't know; one thing I know, that whereas, I was blind, now I see."

John 14:6 Jesus said to him, "I am the way, the truth, and the life. No man comes to the Father, but by Me.

John 8:32 And you shall know the Truth and the Truth shall make you free.

Hebrews 11:6 But without faith, it is impossible to please Him; for he that comes to God must believe that He is, and that He is the rewarder of them that diligently seek Him.

Mark 4:9 And He said to them, "He that has ears to hear, let him hear."

My sixteen-year-old cousin, Christy, lives on a farm where she helps her folks. She expertly drives and backs tractors, farm trucks, cars, and pickups with ease. Her only problem is that she does not have a driver's license, although she is eligible for one. Christy could easily pass the driving test, pay the fees, and get on the family insurance policy, but for whatever reason, she hasn't. Narrow but good roads are there for her use and go right by her home, but until she decides to get her license, she is not allowed to drive on public roads, help her family in more areas, or have insurance for such. The farm products never get to as many in need as they would if Christy could help deliver.

Jesus died for the sins of the whole world (1 John 2:2). That makes everyone eligible for heaven. All of us could be great Christians, but some choose against travelling on the narrow road. We must believe (obey) (John 14:15) in Jesus to be licensed (born again) to receive forgiveness and be heaven-bound and to get our spiritual products to the needy. This is the difference between "Jesus dying for our sins," and "getting forgiveness." There is a lot of "dying for sins" that never gets used. (1 John 1:9; Matthew 22:2–3).

<u>1 John 2:2</u> He is the one who took God's wrath against our sins upon himself, and brought us into fellowship with God; and He is the forgiveness for our sins, and not only ours but all the world's sins.

<u>John 14:15</u> If you love me, keep my commandments.

<u>Matthew 22:2–3</u> The kingdom of heaven is like unto a certain king which made a marriage for his son. And sent forth his servants to call them that were bidden to the wedding, and they would not come.

<u>1 John 1:9</u> If we confess our sins, He is faithful and just to forgive us our sins, and to cleanse us from all unrighteousness.

My neighbor, Les, an insurance salesman, lives in the house just east of me. He and I were talking about my neighbor to the west, Bill Moore. Bill who just returned from a two-week cruise in Europe, and recently purchased a new boat and pickup, looked dejected. Les, the insurance salesman, told me that two years ago Bill Moore dropped all his insurance. Les pleaded with Bill to keep his insurance because someday he would need it (Luke 12:39-40), but Bill insisted he had better use of his resources.

For over a couple of years Bill has not paid any insurance premiums, and has had more fun with the premium money than he ever had mailing it in to the insurance company. However, Bill's wife recently hit a pedestrian in a crosswalk. When they got home from Europe, they found an upstairs water pipe broken which damaged carpeting, flooring, big-screen tv, appliances, etc. (Proverbs 13:15)

Since Les was in insurance, Bill asked if Les could get him insurance for these losses considering Bill had had insurance for many, many years before deciding to cancel (Matthew 10:22), and he had been to Les's house dozens of times- even ate with Les. Also, Bill Moore reminded Les that he had never really spoken derogatorily against insurance.

Sadly, the answer Les had to give was the expected, "No". (Matthew 7:21-23, Revelation 20:15, Galatians 6:7)

To the neighbors it appeared that Mr. Moore had more than Les, but in the end Les had more. (Mark 8:36, Mark 10:31, Matthew 6: 19-20)

**Luke 12:39-40 TLB** Everyone would be ready for Him if they knew the exact hour of His return – just as they would be ready for the thief if they knew when he was coming. So be ready all the time. For, I, the Son of Man of Glory will come when least expected.

**Proverbs 13:15** Good understanding gives favor; but the way of the transgressor is hard.

Matthew 10:22 For it is not you that speak, but the Spirit of your heavenly Father which speaks in you.

Matthew 7:21-23 Not everyone that says unto me, "Lord, Lord, shall enter into the kingdom of heaven; but he that does the will of My Father which is in heaven. Many will say to Me in that day, 'Lord, Lord, have we not prophesied in Your name; and in Your name cast out devils; and in Your name done many wonderful works?'" And then I will profess to them, "I never knew you; depart from Me you that do iniquity."

Revelation 20:15 And whosoever was not found written in the book of life was cast into the lake of fire.

Galatians 6:7 Be not deceived; God is not mocked: for whatsoever a man sows that shall he also reap.

Mark 8:36 For what shall it profit a man if he shall gain the whole world, and lose his own soul.

Mark 10:31 But many that are first shall be last; and the last first.

Matthew 6:19-20 Lay not up for yourselves treasures on earth where moth and rust does corrupt, and where thieves break through and steal. But lay up for yourselves treasures in heaven where neither moth nor rust does corrupt; and where thieves do not break through and steal.

Addiction

When my dad was a teenager, his father who owned a lion, brought him a lion cub. At first Dad was cautious after seeing the claws and teeth. Dad knew all the problems his parents had with his dad's lion.

As the lion and Dad grew, they became friends and spent many hours playing together. Often the lion would hide. Dad would walk by and unexpectedly the lion would pounce on him. Dad, despite a few scratches and bruises, had fun.

As a teenager, Dad acquired friends who were fascinated with the lion and encouraged them to buy one. Playing with the near full-grown lion gave many a teenager a feeling of manhood. Every picture taken of them showed the lion and how much fun they were having.

Dad became acquainted with other lion owners and met occasionally in a sort of unincorporated club at local establishments. Stories of lion bites, ER visits, chasing lions, lion attacks, police involvement, laughing at disgruntled, naive neighbors and bragging about how many lions they could tame, were the usual topics. Seldom would anyone speak of Dad without mentioning the lion.

As a newly-wed, Mom accepted the lion because it was such a part of Dad's life. Although she loved Dad, she did not want the lion. She didn't think it would cost much, and Dad certainly wouldn't keep it nor would he attend many nightly meetings once they started a family. The lion would drop significantly on the family priority list.

After my brother and I were born, Mom stayed home with us while Dad never missed a lion-owner club meeting often coming home late with lion marks. With the lion eating more, the household budget began to tighten, Mom and Dad's arguing increased. Mom insisted the lion must go. Dad refused. Mom would confront Dad with loving the lion more than his family.

The lion didn't bother my brother and me as long as he was content. One time my brother asked Dad if he would take him camping. The lion viciously attacked my brother We all have scars from the lion's attacks with my dad having the most, and we have the awful memories of what the lion did to us. When Dad would come home after a lion attack, we would clean him, bandage his wounds, and lie to friends about how Dad got the wounds. We loved Dad when he wasn't with the lion.

As Dad proved to us his own pleasure was more important than we were, hungered for the love and attention Dad gave to the lion. Mom wasn't happy with the lion; Dad wasn't happy without the lion. Dad accused Mom of not wanting him to be happy. I remember thinking; isn't that like the patient accusing the surgeon of not wanting the patient to be well.

Dad continued spending more time with the lion and other lion-club owners than he did with us. Mom hardly smiled. Our junky pickup would breakdown which would make Dad angry. If we asked for something, he reminded us that he was driving an old junky pickup. When church or school activities came, we lied as we made excuses for Dad's absences.

No one even mentions our lion to us anymore. They know why our family struggles. Mom's unhappy; we are lying for the one we love. Dad can't see beyond the lion. Everything is filtered through the lion. The lion? As long as it's fed first, it's fine.

Through the years some of Dad's best friends have died at the paws of their lions. Some die while transporting the lion while others die from lion injuries accumulated through the years. However, all eventually show the scars including their family members. You don't have to own a lion to have the scars.

Today, Dad brought home a lion for my brother saying it's about time he had one. And me, I'm dating a guy, whose Dad belongs to the same lion-owners' club as my dad, and eventually, he plans to get one himself.

I heard a song with the line, *"I Want a Girl Just Like the Girl That Married Dear Old Dad."* Well, "I want a boy just like the boy that married dear old mom" (II Corinthians 6: 14). I've been brought up in a lion-centered home. I don't know how to live in a family without a lion. Besides, the lion will be such a part of my husband's life. It won't cost much. And after we start a family, I'm sure he won't keep it or attend many lion-owner meetings. After all, family priorities will come first.

I sometimes wonder. Is there such a thing as a lion-tamer? (Luke 19:10) From my experiences a real lion-tamer must be just a fantasy. Who could stand up to a lion and break this family cycle?

The men in my life talk about how brave they are, but none has the courage to defend his family from a lion. And me, well, I guess I want someone else to break the cycle when I am just as guilty not breaking it. I've never seen, a lion tamer; no one has ever told me about one (Romans 10:14). I'm so tired of lions. Does life have to be this hard (Matthew 11:28, John 10:10)?

<u>2 Corinthians 6:14</u> Be you not unequally yoked together with unbelievers: for what fellowship have righteousness with unrighteousness; and what communion has light with darkness?

<u>Luke 19:10</u> For the Son of man is come to seek and to save that which is lost.

<u>Romans 10:14</u> How then shall they call on Him in whom they have not believed? And how shall they believe in Him whom they have not heard? And how shall they hear without a preacher?

<u>Matthew 11:28</u> Come to me all you that labor and are heavy laden, and I will give you rest.

John 10:10 The thief comes to steal, and to kill, and to destroy: I am come that they might have life, and that they might have it more abundantly.

A primitive tribal member came to the USA. While on his first visit, he became enamored with lights in the hostess's house. Bright lights, floor lights, table lights, ceiling lights, and Tiffany-colored lights were throughout the mansion and even lights outside. During his visit the shaman collected a variety of light fixtures to show his fellow tribal members that darkness can be overcome.

Back home the shaman set up the light fixtures for all to see. As the beautiful fixtures sparkled in the daylight, the natives marveled at his beautiful possessions. To show his countrymen that darkness can be overcome, he invited them to return that night for a spectacular display. After dark as all were gathered, the shaman flipped the switches. Much to his surprise the lights did not come on as no one had explained to him about electricity (John 15:1, 4-5).

John 15:1,4-5 I am the true vine and my Father is the husbandman. Abide in Me, and I in you. As the branch cannot bear fruit by itself, except it abide in the vine; no more can you except you abide in Me.

Three men were stranded for years on an ocean island. One day the men found a bottle had washed onto shore. They popped the cork and a genie came out. After the genie sincerely thanked them for freeing her, she granted each islander one wish.

The first one wanted to be home with his family. Poof! He was gone. The second wanted to be driving his new Corvette in his hometown with a million dollars in his pocket. Poof! He was gone. The third islander was a loving but a "pickle shy of a happy meal" sort of fellow. Saddened by the departure of his only friends for the past several years, he said, "Gee, I miss them already. I wish they were back here with me!" Poof!

Mark 3:21 When His friends heard what was happening, they came to try to take Him home with them. "He is out of his mind," they said.

Liv John 2:24-25 But Jesus didn't trust them, for He knew mankind to the core. No one needed to tell Him how changeable human nature is!

Matthew 16: 22-23 Then Peter took Him and began to rebuke Him saying, "Be it far from Thee, Lord; this shall not be unto You." But He turned and said to Peter, "Get thee behind Me, Satan. You are an offense to Me: for you savor not the things that be of God, but those that be of man."

Matthew 21:9 And the multitudes that went before, and that followed, cried, saying, "Hosanna to the Son of David: blessed be He that cometh in the name of the Lord. Hosanna in the highest."

Matthew 27:22 Pilate said to them, "What shall I do then with Jesus which is called Christ?" They all said to him, "Let Him be crucified."

DEATH

If tears were stair steps and sorrows a lane,

I'd march right up to heaven and take you home again.

For years I have deprived myself of some of life's pleasures as I saved for my dream home in the perfect climate. Others scoffed as I refused to spend my time on frivolous temporary pleasures. (Hebrews 11:25) I'm not complaining as my life has been joyous despite life's disappointments, tragedies, and usual pains. (Philippines 4:12-13)

Last spring I retired, said, "Good-bye," to my family and friends and moved to my new residence. It wasn't easy leaving loved ones, but eventually, they will have the opportunity to come and see my wonderful place.

My daughter misses me and wants me to *come home*. She cries when she thinks of me. Although her tears are selfish as I know she is thinking of her missing me and not of the happiness I am enjoying, I am honored that she misses me.

I trust she will make the necessary preparations to come where I am. When she comes to my new residence and sees for herself that this place is more wonderful than anyone could believe, she will understand why I am staying here even if I could return. She must believe that my returning to her is not the answer, but her coming here is. (Revelation 21: 4-7, John 14:2-3)

If you could only see me now, our prayers have been answered.

The healing that had been delayed has finally arrived.

If you could only see me now, I'm walking on streets of gold.

You'd know I've seen His face,

You'd know the pain's erased,

You wouldn't want me to leave this place,

if you could only see me now.

My trials worked out for my good, and brought Him glory when I misunderstood.

Though we have had our sorrows, they could not compare with what Jesus had in store for me no language can share.

If you could only see me now, I'm walking on streets of gold and standing tall and whole.

<u>Hebrews 11:25 TLB</u> choosing rather to suffer affliction with the people of God than to enjoy the pleasures of sin for a season.

<u>Philippians 4:12 TLB</u> I know how to live with almost nothing or with everything. I have learned the secret of contentment in every situation, whether it be a full stomach or hunger, plenty or want. I can do all things through Christ which strengthens me.

<u>Revelation 21:4,7</u> He will wipe away all tears from their eyes, and there shall be no more death, or sorrow, or crying, or pain. All of that has gone forever. Everyone who conquers will inherit all these blessings, and I will be his God and he will be my son.

<u>John 14:2-3</u> In My Father's house are many mansions. If it were not so, I would have told you. I go to prepare a place for you. And if I go and prepare a place for you, I will come again and receive you unto Myself: that where I am, there you may be also.

If you don't know how to die, then you don't know how to live.

<u>Matthew 24:13</u> But he that shall endure to the end, the same shall be saved.

Galatians 2:20 *I am crucified with Christ: nevertheless I live; yet not I, but Christ lives in me and the life I now live in the flesh, I live by the faith of the Son of God, who loved me and gave Himself for me.*

Philippians 1:21 *For me to live is Christ, and to die is gain.*

Romans 6:16-17 TLB *Don't you realize you can choose your own master? You can choose sin (with death) or else obedience (with acquittal). The one to whom you offer yourself- he will take you and be your master and you will be his slave.*

2 Corinthians 6:2 TLB *For God says, "Your cry came to me at a favorable time when the doors of welcome were wide open. I helped you on a day when salvation was being offered. Right now God is ready to welcome you. Now is the day of salvation.*

My neighbor, Julie, after high school graduation, went to trade school for 3 years, undergraduate school for 4 years, graduate school for 2 years, is now enrolled in a 4-year medical program which requires an additional 4-year residency requirement.

She and her husband happily announced to her parents that she is pregnant and will delay her doctorate degree until the child is of school age. Julie, a perennial honor roll student, is always a favorite with her professors and friends.

Her parents are frustrated and label her as a "professional student" who may never enter her career. They can't understand how she turned out this way.

I found all this out when I visited them about our church's many outreach activities. Although Julie's parents have faithfully attended church services and Bible studies for years, church outreach never came at the opportune time, and as of now they have never participated; hopefully next year. You might say they are "stalkers" of Jesus as they stay a safe distance away observing Him, yet never encountering Him. (Proverbs 22:6, James 1: 22-24) Commitment is never convenient.

__Proverbs 22:6__ Train up a child in the way he should go, and when he is old he will not depart from it.

__James 1:22-24__ But be ye doers of the word and not hearers only, deceiving your own selves. For if any be a hearer of the word, and not a doer, he is like unto a man beholding his natural face in a glass: For He beholds himself and goes his way and straightway forgets what manner of man he is.

Are you a "stalker" of Jesus as you stay a safe distance away observing Him, yet never encountering Him. (Revelation 3:20)

__Revelation 3:20__ Behold I stand at the door and knock: if any man hear my voice, and open the door, I will come in to him, and sup with him, and he with Me.

The Waiting Room

I haven't been feeling well for quite some time; nothing serious, in my opinion, just no energy, lethargic. (Matthew 11:28-30) Life seems to be losing its luster. I go to parties, entertainment events, drink a few, eat a lot with friends. All seems to help for awhile. But, by morning, I'm back to my old self (Hebrews 11:25).

I have some friends in the medical field, "real health fanatics", who have encouraged me to visit with the doctor. Fanatics, you know the kind, regular doctor appointments, healthy exercise, proper eating, etc. My opinion of fanatics is that if you are not careful, they will change your whole life style (Psalms 51:10). I don't want a new lifestyle.

I just want my present life with happiness, no loneliness, and not craving something that I don't even know what it is. Maybe I need a career change, or new diet, or medication, or new friends, or new hobby, or, or, or … All I know is that I'm tired of being apathetic, tired of this imbalance, tired of being tired (Matthew 6:33). Like I said, "I don't think it's serious." Maybe it's just a stage of life everyone goes through, or maybe this is all there is to life. Now that's a frightening thought!

Several weeks ago, at the urging of one of my health-fanatic friends, I decided to go with him to his doctor appointment. I sat in the waiting room while my friend saw the doctor. There were the usual pieces of reading material dealing with self-help health issues, such as "Health Today", "Health Tomorrow", "Health Forever;" all good if you need it, but I don't. I'm not <u>that</u> sick.

As we left, my friend asked me how I felt. I think he thought I saw the doctor. I said, 'Same as ever." He encouraged me to make an appointment to see the doctor as soon as possible because in his opinion, my lingering illness is serious and wearing me down. He thinks I should be enjoying life, not tolerating it.

I decided to return, and for the last few weeks I have gone to the doctor's office once a week. I sit in the waiting room for an hour with other patients, some look sick, some don't. However, when the nurse says the doctor wants to see me, I go home.

Possibly, I could get a sickness that other waiting-room occupants have, but sitting in the waiting room hasn't been that bad. I've met some really nice loving people who have invited me to dinner, hospital charity events, and even asked me to help with some of the functions. They give me sympathy for my illness as well as helpful health tips on other ailments. Sympathy is soothing, but like a lot of other things, it doesn't cure. They seem genuinely interested in me, and encourage me to see the doctor, but they aren't the doctor.

From the waiting room conversations, I believe the doctor is legit because those who have been cured speak highly of him (John 9:25). Tell them your problem, and they are not hesitant to tell you about his curing abilities. Me, I can tell what others say about him, but I have no personal experience, therefore, it's not as easy for me to testify on his behalf.

After visiting with others at the doctor's clinic, I realize I'm not the only one who comes, but never sees the doctor. You can always tell them from the others by the answers they give to the questions: "What has the doctor done for you?" Or, "Would you trust the doctor to operate on you?" There are many theories on being healthy, but when you get to the operating room that separates the real doctor from the charlatans. To me, it's seems imperative that you know whom the real doctor is (John 17:3). Some in the waiting room need a doctor as their injuries are obvious.

They want the doctor to sew the wound and stop the pain. They don't want preventative medicine (Lord), just an emergency doctor (Savior) who can patch the wound and get them back to doing whatever it was they were doing that caused the incident.

They want a Savior, not a Lord. Everyone needs a Savior. However, the more Jesus is your Lord, the less you need Him as Savior. (Hebrews 5:12-14, I Corinthians 3:2, James 1:22)

Another waiting-room group is the majority. Just as they leave the doctor's clinic with their prescription in hand, they toss the prescription into the wind. You can't believe how many prescriptions are scattered on the front lawn, along the curb, and in the trees. Why would you seek his healing, then not take the prescriptions? If you think that is incredible, let me tell you the rest of the story. They'll be back next week for another prescription and do the same with it! When their illness painfully progresses, they will complain about the doctor! They just must enjoy the waiting room fellowship.

I always feel safe in the doctor's office, but shortly after leaving, the safe feeling disappears, and I'm back to my usual self.

During last week's visit, I met a person whose friends told him to first see the doctor, then, he would get healthy. He wanted to skip seeing the doctor and just get healthy. (Matthew 6:33)

Finally, he consented to step one. He saw the doctor, got the diagnosis and did nothing about it. He claims the doctor wanted to perform heart surgery causing him severe pain and permanently changing his lifestyle (Galatians 5: 22-24).

Surgery, lifestyle change did not make me feel so good. How could a loving, compassionate doctor want to do heart surgery to a poor innocent over-weight, self-indulgent, shovel-shy, wife-beating alcoholic who "innocently" got hooked on drugs? Makes you wonder about the doctor's competency, and compassion, doesn't it!

The poor man's condition worsened, so he had his wife drive him to the doctor to ask the proverbial question, "Doc, is there any other way?" (John 14:6)

He told the doctor he believed the doctor was a doctor; that he had not really said too much bad about him; that he had driven by the clinic many times and waved; and that he regularly went to the clinic every December and April. He thought the doctor could cure him; he just didn't want the operation (Revelation 3:16). I guess I'm like that. I have always wanted to play the piano; I just don't want to take the lessons.

Another patient said that the doctor lovingly took him in the condition he was, but loved him too much to leave him that way. Needless to say, if you were to ask this man, or the other patients, like me, who never see the doctor but just sit in the waiting room, "Is the doctor any good?" we would have to confess, "He really hasn't helped us." Of course, those who saw him and took his advice would, I'm sure, have a much different opinion.

Jim Shoulders, the world's greatest bull-rider of yesteryear stated, "Opinions are just like the back of the lap, everyone's got one." It's probably wise to ask the right person for a second opinion. (John 7:17)

I've been going to the doctor now for several weeks, and each time the nurse informs me the doctor wants to speak to me, I leave. It's getting easier. At first it was hard to leave without seeing him, but now, not so much (Mark 7:9). I think it's a lot like getting a callous. A blister hurts, but after continuous rubbing, the callous develops, and the pain lessens.

Talk in the waiting room is that the Doc is quite a guy; came from a poor laboring family, pretty much self-taught, great teacher, miraculous healer and known world-wide. Despite medical journals that say he has healed blindness, revived the lifeless, cured the insane, and healed a variety of cardio and neurological cases, how do I know if he can heal me? Maybe his specialty is trauma cases, and I don't think I'm that sick (Romans 6:23).

Despite many patients, he is seeking to expand his patient list (2 Peter 3:9) and still makes house calls (Revelation 3:20). He came knocking at my door the other day, but I didn't let him in. I don't mind people seeing me at his office, but what would the neighbors say if they saw him at my house (Matthew 10:33). How embarrassing for one of my neighbors to come over coughing and wheezing and find a doctor in my house.

I just don't understand why he wants me when he has so many other patients. I called to ask him why all of a sudden he cares about me. He told me that many tears ago he was caring for me even before I was born (Job 31:15). He said he has always cared and has set up many, many appointments to see me. I kind of remember, but I thought it was junk mail and tossed them.

He said ever since I was born he has known about my condition. Then he asked me why I wouldn't talk with him. That's when I realized why I thought it was so strange why he cared about me. I always thought I had to show an interest in someone first before that person would care about me (1 John 4:19). He cared for me, and I didn't even know him nor reciprocate his love. I've never known anyone like him, so I thought he was weird when all along I was the problem.

My health-fanatic friends found my symptoms in their medical handbook, and my illness, which I thought wasn't serious, is terminal (Romans 6:23). Unless the doctor treats my heart, my curable condition will worsen eventually causing death.

They ask why I would want to be miserable when I can have an abundant life (John 10:10). I don't know anything about the abundant life; therefore, maybe I should stick with what I know, the pain of dying. Maybe I should check into the abundant life thing? Maybe I should try being content with temporary pain relief as I die?

There's the doorbell. What if it's the doctor again? Should I let him in? If you were dying, what would you do?

Matthew 11:28-30 Take my yoke upon you, and learn of me; for I am meek and lowly of heart and you shall find rest for your souls; for my yoke is easy, and my burden is light.

Hebrews 11:25 Choosing rather to suffer affliction with the people of God, than to enjoy the pleasures of sin for a season.

Psalms 51:10 Create in me a clean heart O God, and renew a right spirit within me.

Matthew 6:33 But seek you first the kingdom of God and His righteousness, and all these things shall be added unto you.

John 9:25 He answered and said, "Whether He be a sinner or no, I know not: one thing I know that, whereas, I was blind, and now I see."

John 17:13 And now come I to you and these things speak I in the world, that they might have My joy fulfilled in themselves

Hebrews 5:12-14 TLB You have been Christians a long time now, and you ought to be teaching others, but instead you have dropped back to the place where you need someone to teach you all over again the very principles in God's Word. You are like babies who can drink only milk, not old enough for solid food. And when a person is still living on milk, it shows he isn't very far along in the Christian life, and doesn't know much about the difference between right and wrong. He is still a baby Christian! You will never be able to eat solid Spiritual food and understand the deeper things of God's Word until you become better Christians and learn right from wrong by practicing doing right.

1 Corinthians 3:2 I have fed you with milk, and not with meat because you were not able to bear it; neither yet now are you able.

James 1:22 But be ye doers of the word and not hearers only.

Galatians 5:22-24 But the fruit of the Spirit is love, joy, peace, longsuffering, gentleness, goodness, faithfulness, meekness, self-control: against such there is no law. And those who have nailed their natural evil desires to His cross, have crucified them there.

John 14:6 Jesus said unto him, "I am the way, the truth, and the life; no man cometh unto the Father, but by Me."

Revelation 3:16 So then because you are lukewarm, and neither cold nor hot, I will spit you out of My mouth.

John 7:17 If any of you really determines to do God's will, then you will certainly know whether My teaching is from God or merely from man.

Mark 7:9 And He said to them, "Full well you reject the commandment of God, that you may keep your own tradition.

Romans 6:23 For the wages of sin is death, but the gift of God is eternal life through Jesus Christ our Lord.

2 Peter 3:9 And the Lord is not slack concerning His promise, as some men count slackness; but is longsuffering toward us; not willing that any should perish, but that all should come to repentance.

Revelation 3:20 Behold, I stand at the door and knock; if any man hears My voice and opens the door, I will come in to him, and will sup with him, and he with Me.

Matthew 10:33 But whosoever shall deny Me before men; him shall I deny before My Father which is in heaven.

Job 31:15 Did not He that made me in the womb make him? And did not one fashion us in the womb?

1 John 4:19 We love Him because He first loved us.

John 10:10 The thief comes to steal, and to kill, and to destroy: I am come that they might have life, and that they might have it more abundantly.

An apathetic congregation becomes a crowd.

Revelation 3: 15-16 I know your works that you are neither cold nor hot. I would you were cold or hot. So then because you are lukewarm and neither cold nor hot, I will spit you out of my mouth.

Money is a great servant, but a poor king.

Matthew 6:24 No man can serve two masters: for either he will hate the one and love the other; or else he will hold to the one and despise the other. You cannot serve God and mammon.

Wealth can be a window in which we see God, or a mirror in which we see ourselves.

1Timothy 6:10 For the love of money is the root of all evil; which while some have coveted after they have erred from the faith and pierced themselves through with many sorrows.

James 1:23-24 For if any be a hearer of the word, and not a doer, he is like unto a man beholding his natural face in a glass: For he beholds himself and goes his way and straightway forgets what manner of man he is.

Adversity is a great teacher: prosperity not so much.

<u>I Peter 4:12-14</u> Beloved think it not strange concerning the fiery trial which is to try you, as though some strange thing happened to you. But rejoice inasmuch as you are partakers of Christ's sufferings; that when His glory shall be revealed, you may be glad also with exceeding joy. If you be reproached for the name of Christ, happy are you; for the spirit of glory and of God rests upon you; on their part He is evil spoken of, but on your part He is glorified.

We buy things we don't need with money we don't have to impress people we don't like.

<u>Luke 20:46-47 TLB</u> Beware of the experts in religion for they love to parade in dignified robes and to be bowed to by the people as they walk along the street. And how they love the seats of honor in the synagogues and at religious festivals! But even while they are praying long prayers with great outward piety, they are planning schemes to cheat widows out of their property. Therefore, God's heaviest sentences await these men.

Cutting up uncontrolled credit cards is the purist form of healthy plastic surgery.

<u>Romans 13:7-8 TLB</u> Pay everyone whatever you ought to have: pay your taxes and import duties gladly, obey those over you, and give honor and respect to all those to whom it is due. Pay all your debts except the debt of love for others – never finish paying that! For if you love them, you will be obeying all of God's laws, fulfilling all His requirements.

Don't trade in your spiritual diamonds for earthly sparkling glass.

John 12:43 For they loved the praise of men more than the praise of God.

There is a difference between adore and a door. "Oh, come let us adore Him!"

Revelation 3:20 Behold, I stand at the door and knock; if any man hears My voice and opens the door, I will come in to him, and will sup with him, and he with Me.

I decided to accept my friend's invitation (Romans 10: 14) to attend the stage production of "World," based on a true-life story. Since this was my first theater experience, I eagerly walked to the theater in a large crowd. To my surprise many walked past the theater missing the opportunity to see the production for whatever reason (Matthew 7:14).

Inside the theater everybody seemed to be buzzing with excitement as they discussed the play. Some had seen it before and were eager to see it again. Others, like me, were viewing it for the first time.

We took our seats and waited for Scene 1. After several minutes some, even with excellent seats, got up and left impatiently. They mumbled disappointingly about nothing happening. Some were convinced that the play was over (Isaiah 40:31). For those of us staying, the anticipation grew.

Finally, the curtains opened, and Scene 1 began with a typical day in the life of a typical person. The plot begins and conflict enters into the main character's life. Scene 1 ends with a developing plot.

During the intermission some were not interested in the play's outcome and decided to find something more exciting. Others thought they knew the tragic ending because the same thing had happened to them.

In Scene 2 emotions increase as the main character's situations sadly increase to the point that the audience collectively thinks, "I'm glad that isn't me!" (I Corinthians 10:13)

Scene 2 ends as several leave whispering that the tragedy is too emotional for them and believing nothing can be done. (Luke 1:37, Jeremiah 32:27, Matthew 27:42)

Scene 3 continues with sadness (I Peter 4:12-13), but the main character begins to overcome, and one realizes that it was through the conflicts that strength was developed (II Corinthians 12:10). Without the devoted friend and the main character's strength, others would not have benefitted. The trail had been blazed for others travelling the same or similar journeys. Others did not wish tragic conflict on the character, but rejoiced that they had witnessed an over comer (John 16:33).

As the curtain came down on Scene 3 people tearfully applauded and just sat in their seats overcome by a masterful play and wanting to know the director. I had heard about this writer, but until I had experienced his complete work, I had no idea of his greatness. Regretfully, I remembered all who impatiently left early and never witnessed the last scene. (Revelation 21:3-4)

***Romans 10:14 TLB** But how shall they ask Him to save them unless they believe in Him? And how can they believe in Him if they have never heard about Him? And how can they hear about him unless someone tells them?*

Matthew 7:14 But straight is the gate and narrow is the way, which leads to life; and few there be that find it.

Isaiah 40:31 But they that wait upon the Lord shall renew their strength; they shall mount up with wings as eagles; they shall run and not be weary; and they shall walk and not faint.

1 Corinthians 10:13 There is no temptation taken you but such is common to man: but God is faithful, who will not suffer you to be tempted above that you are able; but will with the temptation also make a way to escape, that you may be able to bear it.

Luke 1:37 For with God nothing shall be impossible.

Jeremiah 32:27 Behold, I am the Lord, the God of all flesh. Is there anything too hard for Me?

Matthew 27:42 He saved others; himself He cannot save. If He be the King of Israel, let Him now come down from the cross, and we will believe Him.

1 Peter 4:12-13 Beloved think it not strange concerning the fiery trial which is to try you, as though some strange thing happened to you. But rejoice inasmuch as you are partakers of Christ's sufferings; that when His glory shall be revealed, you may be glad also with exceeding joy.

2 Corinthians 12:10 Therefore, I take pleasure in infirmities, in reproaches, in necessities, in persecutions, in distresses for Christ's sake: for when I am weak, then am I strong.

John 16:33 These things have I spoken to you that in Me you might have peace. In the world you will have tribulation: but be of good cheer; I have overcome the world.

Revelation 21:3-4 *And I heard a great voice out of heaven saying, "Behold, the tabernacle of God is with men, And He will dwell with them, and they shall be His people, and God Himself shall be with them, and be their God. And God shall wipe away all tears from their eyes; and there shall be no more death, neither sorrow, nor crying, neither shall there be any more pain: for the former things are passed away.*

At the hospital I visited an acquaintance who denies God's guidance, but not His existence, just His help. Although his injuries were substantial, he was no longer in intensive care. After the usual questions about his present condition, I asked how the accident happened. Bill told me he was t-boned at one of the city's busy intersections. I asked, inquisitively, if the other person had run a red light. Much to my surprise, Bill stated she had the green light.

Since Bill works in the city's traffic control maintenance department, I assumed he, if anyone, would religiously watch for all traffic signs.

Then Bill explained to me that he doesn't believe in following traffic regulations or signs (Titus 1:16). He refuses to obey speed limits, stoplights, or any other regulatory sign because he doesn't understand why they are needed! (Matthew 23: 3-4) He just pays speeding tickets (considers them as buying a speeding permit!) and observes intersections before driving through despite ignoring the stop sign or red light (Titus 1:16). He's driven through many intersections without incident. Needless to say, because of his driving record, Bill, who drives a damaged pickup, has no insurance or driver's license. He claims he has saved thousands through this practice.

What about your family? Do you allow them to ride with you? (Luke 16:15) "Of course," was his reply. Did the lady who hit you get injured? Bill confessed she was still in intensive care, but she should have been more observing when approaching an intersection.

Someone needs to teach her how to drive. Will this incident change your thinking? "Why would it? I have ignored many traffic signals and not gotten hurt," was Bill's reply. (Proverbs 13:15, Job 4:8)

Titus 1:16 They profess that they know God; but in works they deny Him. They are rotten and disobedient, worthless so far as doing good is concerned.

Matthew 23:3-4 Of course you should obey their every whim! It may be all right to do what they say, but above anything else, don't follow their example. For, they don't do what they tell you to do.

Luke 16:15 And He said to them, "You are they which justify yourselves before men; but God knows your hearts; for that which is highly esteemed among men is abomination in the sight of God.

Proverbs 13:15 Good understanding gives favor; but the way of the transgressor is hard.

Job 4:8 Even as I have seen, they that plow iniquity and sow wickedness, reap the same.

Since this morning I am officially retired, I decided to go this afternoon to withdraw my savings, buy my dream retirement home, and live happily ever after.

I saw the banker with whom I had done business for many years, explained my intentions, and asked for the savings withdrawal.

The banker, whom I know really likes me, checked the ledger and sadly returned informing me he could not find any savings account in my name (Matthew 7:21-23, Revelation 20:15).

"Impossible," was my reply! I've been a good customer of this bank for years. Personally, I have known every loan officer this bank has ever had. I've borrowed money to buy my first car, my houses, to support my family when we struggled (Matthew 6:19-20). Although now closed, I even had a savings account for my daughter's college.

With regret, the banker told me he was well aware of the many times I had asked them for money, but loans and savings accounts weren't the same and no savings/investment bank officer recognized my name. He even remembered loaning me money when my credit wasn't the best (Romans 5:8). He reminded me that his son had co-signed a note with me (1 Peter 3:18) and had sold everything he had to repay the loan when I couldn't.

Many times he and his son had begged me to start a savings account which I thought about doing at a later time. (II Corinthians 6:2). They had reminded me that the sooner I started an account the better it would be for me.

I informed the banker that I had gotten several people to start banking with him, and they had started savings accounts. Many times I had put his banking signs on my classic '69 Corvette and had driven in the local parades advertising for his bank (Matthew 7:22-23). I knew many of his employees as friends, even had some for neighbors. Although we never were socially seen together, I always liked my banker. I had attended many of his free investment meetings, retirement meetings, and money management meetings where the refreshments were deliciously homemade.

I cannot work anymore. I need the money. How could a banker with so much money be so cruel? Why would he let me get in this situation if he really liked me? Obviously, it's the banker's fault, and now I have to live with the results (Galatians 6:7).

Matthew 7:21-23 Not everyone that says to Me, "Lord, Lord," shall enter into the kingdom of heaven; but he that does the will of My Father which is in heaven. Many shall say unto Me in that day, Lord, Lord, have we not prophesied in Thy name? And in Thy name have we not cast out devils; and in Thy name done many wonderful works? And then will I profess unto them, "I never knew you. Depart from Me you that do iniquity."

Revelation 20:15 And whosoever was not found written in the book of life was cast into the lake of fire.

Matthew 6:19-20 Lay not up for yourselves treasures upon earth, where moth and rust doth corrupt, and where thieves break through and steal. Lay up for yourselves treasures in heaven where neither moth nor rust corrupt, and where thieves do not break through and steal.

Romans 5:8 But God commended His love toward us, in that while we were yet sinners, Christ died for us.

1Peter 3:18 For Christ has once suffered for all sins, the just for the unjust, that He might bring us to God, being put to death in the flesh, but to live by the Spirit.

2 Corinthians 6:2 For He said, "I have heard you in the time accepted, and in the day of salvation have I helped you: behold now is the accepted time: behold now is the day of salvation.

Matthew 7:22-23 Many shall say unto Me in that day, Lord, Lord, have we not prophesied in Thy name? And in Thy name have we not cast out devils; and in Thy name done many wonderful works? And then will I profess unto them, "I never knew you. Depart from Me you that do iniquity."

Galatians 6:7 Be not deceived God is not mocked: whatsoever a man sows, that shall he also reap.

Planning for the future is not a sin; planning for the future without God is.

Luke 12:19-21 And I will say to myself, you have much goods laid up for many years; take your ease, eat, drink, and be merry. But God said unto him, "You fool, this night your soul shall be required of you: then whose shall these things be which you have provided.

Luke 14:28 For which of you intending to build a tower sitteth not down first and counteth the cost whether he have sufficient to finish it.

You cannot take it with you, but you can send it on ahead.

Luke 12:33 TLB Sell what you have and give to the needy. This will fatten your purses in heaven! And the purses of heaven have no rips or holes in them. Your treasures there will never disappear; no thief can steal them; no moth can eat them.

1 Timothy 6:19 TLB By doing this they will be laying up for themselves real treasures in heaven – it is the only safe investment for eternity! And they will be living a fruitful Christian life down here as well.

You may be from the same city as the World Series Champions, cheered for them, gone to all the games, hit many home runs in your back yard, but unless you are a team member, you will not get a share of the World Series reward.

Luke 13:26-27 Then shall you begin to say, "We have eaten and drunk in your presence, and you have taught in our streets." But He will say, "I tell you, I know you not who you are; depart from Me all you workers of iniquity."

If you won't play for the winning team, why would you expect to hold the trophy?

Matthew 12:30 He that is not for Me, is against Me; and he that gathers not with me scatters abroad.

2 Timothy 4:7-8 I have fought the good fight, I have finished my course, I have kept the faith. Henceforth, there is laid up for me a crown of righteousness which the Lord, the righteous judge shall give me at that day: and not to me only, but to all them also that love His appearing again.

Don't expect a victory party in hell.

Luke 15:7,10 I say unto you likewise, "Joy shall be in heaven over one sinner that repents, more than over 99 just persons which need no repentance." Likewise, I say to you, "There is joy in the presence of the angels of God over one sinner that repents.

Revelation 20:15 And whosoever was not found written in the book of life was cast into the lake of fire.

God will not allow you to be tempted above what you are able to handle. (1Corinthians 10:12-13) The same can be said for blessings. (1 Corinthians 3:2)

1 Corinthians 10:12-13 So be careful, if you are thinking, "Oh, I would never behave like that" – let this be a warning to you; you may fall into sin. There is no temptation taken you but such as is common to man: but God faithful, who will not suffer you to be tempted above that you are able; but will with the temptation also make a way to escape, that you may be able to bear it.

1 Corinthians 3:2 (spiritually) I have fed you with milk and not with meat, for hitherto you were not able to bear it, neither yet now are you able.

God does not give us what we can't bear; He helps us bear what we are given.

Luke 22:42-43 Saying, "Father, if you are willing, remove this cup from Me: nevertheless, not My will, but yours be done. And there appeared an angel unto Him from heaven strengthening Him.

John 17:15 I pray not that you should take them out of the world, but that you should keep them from evil.

Fiery trials should be your teacher, not your undertaker. (2 Corinthians 12:10, 1 Peter 4:12) If you can't bear the cross, then you can't wear the crown.

2 Corinthians 12:10 Therefore, I take pleasure in infirmities, in reproaches, in necessities, in persecutions, in distresses for Christ's sake: for when I am weak, then am I strong.

1 Peter 4:12-13 Beloved think it not strange concerning the fiery trial which is to try you, as though some strange thing happened to you. But rejoice inasmuch as you are partakers of Christ's sufferings; that when His glory shall be revealed, you may be glad also with exceeding joy.

It's not the fiery trials going away; it's learning how to deal with the trials, that produces peace.

***Philippians 4:11-12** Not that I speak in respect of want: for I have learned in whatsoever state I am therewith to be content I know how to live with almost nothing or with everything. I have learned the secret of contentment in every situation, whether it be a full stomach or hunger, plenty or want. I can do all things through Christ which strengthens me.*

When an idiot (*not a medical term*) becomes a Christian, he is still an idiot (ID10T), just a saved "id10t!" that is blessed.

***Romans 10:13 12:5-7** For whosoever shall call upon the name of the Lord shall be saved. So we being many are one body in Christ, and everyone members one of another. Having then gifts differing according to the grace that is given to us, whether prophesy, let us prophesy according to the proportion of faith.*

***1 Corinthians 12:12,15** Our bodies have many parts, but the many parts make up only one body when they are all put together. So it is with the "body" of Christ. If the foot says, "I am not a part of the body because I am not a hand," that does not make it any less a part of the body.*

The "Dos" and "Don'ts" of the Bible (knowledge of sin) were never meant to save us (Galatians 3:11, 25; Romans 8:1, Ephesians 2:5). The legalist who tries to keep all the "Dos" and "Don'ts" is bogged down in insecurity and frustration for he can never do enough to satisfy the standard of divine righteousness. (Romans 8:3) God's grace redeems us (Romans 3:23-24).

***Galatians 3:11,25 TLB** Consequently, it is clear that no one can ever win God's favor by trying to keep the Jewish laws, because God has said that the only way we can be right in His sight is by faith. As the prophet, Habakkuk says it, "The man who finds life will find it through trusting God."*

Romans 8:1 TLB So there is now no condemnation awaiting those who belong to Christ Jesus.

Ephesians 2:5 Even when we were dead in sins, He has given us back our lives when He raised Christ from the dead – only by grace (undeserved favor) are you saved.

Romans 8:3 For what the law could not do, in that it was weak through the flesh, God sending His own Son in the likeness of sinful flesh, and for sin, condemned sin in the flesh.

Romans 3:23-24 For all have sinned and come short of the glory of God. Being justified freely by His grace through the redemption that is in Christ Jesus.

Our loving God's, "<u>No</u>," is always positive and right. (Luke 22:41-42, Revelation 21:3-4) <u>No</u> more tears, <u>no</u> more death, <u>no</u> sorrow, <u>no</u> crying, <u>no</u> pain.

Luke 22:41-42 And He was withdrawn from them about a stone's cast and kneeled down and prayed, saying, "Father, if you are willing, remove this cup from Me: nevertheless, not My will, but yours be done."

Revelation 21:3-4 And I heard a great voice out of heaven saying, "Behold, the tabernacle of God is with men, And He will dwell with them, and they shall be His people, and God Himself shall be with them, and be their God. And God shall wipe away all tears from their eyes; and there shall be no more death, neither sorrow, nor crying, neither shall there be any more pain: for the former things are passed away.

God's love is the Christian law, therefore, holiness is measured chiefly by Christian love. The *question* is can you love your neighbors and not offer them heaven and the fruits of the Spirit?

Romans 10:13-14 For whosoever shall call upon the name of the Lord shall be saved. But how shall they ask Him to save them unless they believe in Him? And how can they believe in Him if they have never heard about Him? And how can they hear about him unless someone tells them?

Galatians 5:14, 22-24 TLB For the whole law can be summed up in this one command: Love others as you love yourself. But the fruit of the Spirit is love, joy, peace, longsuffering, guidance, goodness, and faithfulness, meekness, self-control; and here there is no control with Jewish laws. Those who belong to Christ have nailed their natural evil desires to His cross and crucified them there.

A time when it is acceptable to spend more than you earn.

Galatians 5:22-25 But the fruit of the Spirit is love, joy, peace, longsuffering, guidance, goodness, and faithfulness, meekness, self-control; and here there is no control with Jewish laws. Those who belong to Christ have nailed their natural evil desires to His cross and crucified them there. If we are now living by the Holy Spirit's power, let us follow the Holy Spirit's leading in every part of our lives.

The Galatians 5:22 fruit tree would not have grown without a loving God, resurrected Savior, and your painful perseverance, faith, and obedience.

<u>Galatians 5:22</u> But the fruit of the Spirit is love, joy, peace, longsuffering, guidance, goodness, and faithfulness, meekness, self-control

<u>John 15:4</u> Abide in Me and I in you. As the branch cannot bear fruit of itself, except it abide in the vine; no more can you, except you abide in Me.

Courtship to marriage is like a fruit catalog picture to what comes up in the garden. One should not be competing, but completing with one's spouse.

<u>Proverbs 14:12</u> Those who follow the right path respect the Lord; those who take the wrong path despise Him.

<u>Galatians 6:7</u> Be not deceived, God is not mocked. Whatsoever a man sows that shall he also reap.

As a reward to successful athletes at various levels who had done exemplary community service, a company provided a week's vacation at a famous island resort. Over the ocean the plane developed engine trouble and went down on the water. As the plane was sinking, those who had not heeded the stewardesses instructions (John 3:3) where the life jackets and emergency exits were located began sinking and screaming. They offered their rings, medals, money, all they had for a life jacket (Mark 8:36).

In the end, only two kinds of people mattered; survivors and non-survivors (Matthew 25:32-34). You may be all-state, all-American, all-world, but if all-heaven is not added to your name, you are not a judgment day survivor.

John 3:3 Jesus answered and said to him, "Verily, verily I say to you, except a man be born again, he cannot see the kingdom of God."

Mark 8:36 For what shall it profit a man, if he shall gain the whole world, and lose his soul?

Matthew 25:32-34 And before Him shall be gathered all nations: and He shall separate them one from another, as a shepherd divides the sheep from the goats. And, He shall set the sheep on His right hand, but the goats on His left. Then shall the king say to them on His right hand, "Come you blessed of my Father, inherit the kingdom prepared for you from the foundation of the world."

Christians are Aliens!

Hebrews 13:14 TLB For this world is not our home; we are looking forward to our everlasting home in heaven.

Not putting on God's armor is no different from a bomb squad member not putting on any protective gear. This shows a disregard for not only personal life, but the lives of family members and those close-by. Those who reject Jesus not only suffer themselves but those near them suffer also.

Ephesians 6:11-12 Put on the whole armor of God that you may stand up against the strategies and deceits of the devil. For we wrestle not against flesh and blood, but the principalities, and against powers against the rulers of the darkness of this world, against spiritual wickedness in high places.

Joshua 24:15 ... but as for me and my house, we will serve the Lord.

Acts 16:14-15 TLB *One of them was Lydia, a saleswoman from Thyatire, a merchant of purple cloth. She was already a worshipper of God and, as she listened to us, the Lord opened her heart, and she accepted all that Paul was saying. She was baptized along with all her household and asked us to be her guests ...*

The Bible is the closet where God's armor is found.

Ephesians 6:13 *Wherefore, take to you the whole armor of God, that you may be able to withstand in the evil day, and having done all, you still will be standing.*

Prayer changes things; usually the one praying.

Ephesians 6:18 TLB *Pray all the time. Ask God for anything in line with the Holy Spirit's wishes. Plead with Him reminding Him of your needs, and keep praying earnestly for all Christians everywhere.*

Refusing to choose is a choice.

John 3:18 *He that believes on Him is not condemned; but he that believes not is condemned already because he has not believed in the name of the only begotten son of God.*

Romans 14:11-12 *For it is written, as I live, says the Lord, "Every knee shall bow to Me, and every tongue shall confess to God. So then every one of us shall give an account of himself to God.*

Mercy rejected (not accepted) becomes condemnation.

John 3:18 *He that believes on Him is not condemned; but he that believes not is condemned already because he has not believed in the name of the only begotten son of God.*

Always grace and peace; never peace then grace. The cross comes before the crown.

2 Peter 1:2 _Grace and peace be multiplied to you through the knowledge of God, and of Jesus our Lord._

Ephesians 2:8,14 _For by grace (unmerited favor) are you saved through faith, and not that of yourselves: it is the gift of God. For Christ, Himself, is our way to peace. He has made peace between us Jews and you Gentiles by making us all one family, breaking down the wall of contempt that used to separate us._

Love produces obedience. Obedience is the product of love not the producer. Obedience is different from law abiding.

John 14:23 _Jesus answered to him, "If a man love Me, he will keep my words; and My Father will love him; and We will come to him, and make our abode with him."_

John 15:10 _If you keep My commandments, you shall remain in my love; even as I have kept My Father's commandments, and remain in His love._

Importance of Easter: Jesus became the _author of eternal salvation_ through the resurrection. Without the resurrection, Jesus was just another lamb on the altar.

Hebrews 5:9 _And Jesus being made perfect, He became the author of eternal salvation unto all them that obey Him._

If you allow Him, God will turn your Calvary, into your Easter. Only God can turn your _mess_ into a _message_, a _test_ into a _testimony_, a _trial_ into a _triumph_, and a _victim_ into a _victory_.

Matthew 5:11-12 Blessed are you when men shall revile you, and persecute you, and shall say all manner of evil against you falsely for My sake. Rejoice and be exceeding glad for great is your reward in heaven: for so persecuted they the prophets which were before you.

John 16:32 Behold the hour comes, yes, is now come, that you will be scattered, every man to his own, and shall leave Me alone: and yet I am not alone, because the Father is with Me.

Jeremiah 32:27 Behold, I am the Lord, the God of all flesh. Is there anything too hard for Me?

The shed blood of Jesus graciously forgives rather than cries for vengeance.

Luke 23:33-34 And when they were come to the place, which is called Calvary, there they crucified Him, and the criminals, one on the right hand and the other on the left. Then said Jesus, "Father, forgive them; for they know not what they do." And they parted His clothing and cast lots.

Hebrews 12:24 TLB And to Jesus himself who has brought us His wonderful new agreement; and to the sprinkled blood which graciously forgives instead of crying out for revenge as the blood of Abel did.

Those who live by faith (Romans 1:17) and die in faith (Mark 13:13) will rejoice (1 Peter 4:13) because of faith.

Romans 1:17 For therein is the righteousness of God revealed from faith to faith, as it is written: the just shall live by faith.

Mark 13:13 And you shall be hated of all men for My name's sake; but he that endures to the end, the same shall be saved.

1 Peter 4:13 But, rejoice inasmuch as you are partakers of Christ's suffering; that when His glory shall be revealed, you may be glad also with exceeding joy.

The difference between a *judge* and a *father*: God the Father (Luke 12:32) God the Judge (Revelation 20:12, 15) When we become Christians, God is no longer our judge, but our Father. (Hebrews 8:12)

Luke 12:32 Fear not, little flock: for it is your Father's good pleasure to give you the kingdom.

Revelation 20:12,15 And I saw the dead, both great and small stand before God; and the books were opened: and another book was opened which is the book of life: and the dead were judged out of those things which were written in the books, according to their works. And whosoever was not found written in the book of life was cast into the lake of fire.

Hebrews 8:12 For I will be merciful to their unrighteousness, and their sins and iniquities will I remember no more.

Jesus was not a martyr. He is a Savior. (1 John 4:14) It is Christ's blood even more than death that implies sacrifice. One may die without being slain, and one may be slain without being a sacrifice. Jesus *willingly* shed His blood. (Luke 22:42, John 19:30, Hebrews 9:22)

1 John 4:14 And we have seen and do testify that the Father sent the Son to be the Savior of the world.

***Luke 22:42** Saying, "Father, if thou be willing, remove this cup from Me. Nevertheless, not My will but thy will be done."*

***John 19:30 TLB** When Jesus had tasted the vinegar, He said, "It is finished," and bowed His head and dismissed His spirit.*

***Hebrews 9:22** And almost all things are by the law purged with blood and without shedding of blood is no remission.*

God's gift to you requires assembly. Be careful how you assemble it. Be vigilant not to worship the gift but the Giver.

***James 1:17** Every good and every perfect gift is from above, and comes down from the Father of lights with Him is no change neither shadow of turning.*

God tests (1 Peter 1:7) and Satan tempts (1 Thessalonians 3:5). Like all good teachers, God gives us a spiritual test to take. Satan tempts us with a cheat sheet. (James 1:13)

***1 Peter 1:7** That the trial of your faith, being much more precious than of gold that perishes though it be tried with fire, might be found unto praise and honor and glory at the appearing of Jesus Christ.*

***1 Thessalonians 3:5** For this cause when I could no longer forbear, I sent to know your faith; lest by some means the tempter have tempted you, and our labor be in vain.*

***James 1:13** Let no man say when he is tempted, "I am tempted by God." For God cannot be tempted with evil, neither tempt He any man.*

Good works is the essential and proper fruit of faith. (James 2:15-17, 26) Faith produces good works, not vice versa.

James 2:15-17,26 If you have a friend who is in need of food and clothing and you say to him, "Well, good-bye and God bless you, stay warm and eat hearty," and then don't give him any clothes or food, what good does that do? So you see, it isn't enough just to have faith. You must also do good to prove you have it. Faith that doesn't show itself by good works is no faith at all – it is dead and useless.

A counterfeit faith is one that does not really concern itself by active participation in the spiritual needs of others.

James 2:26 For as the body without the spirit is dead, so faith without works is dead also.

All prayer is subject to the will of God. James 5:15, Matthew 6:10, Matthew 26:42, John 14:13) Do you think God will give you what you want to serve Satan?

James 5:15 And the prayer of faith shall save the sick, and the Lord shall raise him up; and if he has committed sins, they shall be forgiven.

Matthew 6:10 Thy kingdom come, Thy will be done in earth as it is in heaven.

Matthew 26:42 He went away again the second time and prayed, saying, "O My Father, if this cup may not pass away from Me except I drink it, Thy will be done."

John 14:13 And whatever you shall ask in My name, that will I do that the Father may be glorified in the Son.

Jesus paid debt He didn't owe because we owed a debt we couldn't pay.

1 Peter 2:24 *Who by his own self bare our sins in His own body on the tree, that we, being dead to sins, should live unto righteousness: by whose stripes we are healed.*

In an interview a college coach was asked about recruiting. A certain young athlete he had recruited had been convicted of stealing. Why would he recruit someone who had such a conviction? His reply was, "There is a difference between a mistake and a habit." If a young man makes a mistake, that is one thing, but if it becomes a habit, that is quite another.

1 John 3:6-7, 9 TLB *So if we stay close to Him, obedient to Him, we won't be sinning either; but as for those who keep on sinning, they should realize this: they sin because they have never really known Him or become His. Oh, dear children, don't let anyone deceive you about this: if you are constantly doing what is good, it is because you are good, even as He is. The person who has been born into God's family does not make a practice of sinning, because now God's life is in him; so he cannot keep on sinning, for this new life has been born into him and controls him – he has been born again.*

God doesn't need a lawyer; He needs a witness. (John 4:28-29, 39) The greatest witness is one that is part of the evidence. (John 9:25)

John 4:28-29,39 TLB *The woman then left her water pot and went her way into the city, and said to the men, "Come see a man which told me all things that ever I did. Is not this the Christ." And many Samaritans of that city believed on Him for the saying of the woman which testified, "He told me all that I ever did."*

John 9:25 *He answered and said, "Whether He be a sinner or no, I know not: one thing I know, that, whereas, I was blind, now I see."*

At an airport a commercial pilot's goal is not to leave passengers behind, but to pick up his customers. The customers at the airport can choose with their own free wills for which destinations to buy a ticket. Despite how great the pilot is at getting his passengers safely to the destination, the choice is theirs.

It's not the pilot's fault they decided not to buy tickets on his plane. The scheduled destinations were clearly listed and advertised, everyone had the opportunity to read them, people excitedly told of the plane's destination, and tickets could have easily been purchased to the delight of the airline. Some people mistakenly believe other planes are going to the same location (John 14:6). Unfortunately, once the plane leaves the runway, it's too late to board.

Jesus is coming again (Matthew 24:30-31) and His goal (2 Peter 3:9) is not to leave people behind, but to take his ticketed (Romans 10:9) passengers, to their designated destination (Matthew 25:34). The Bible clearly lists the destinations (Matthew 25:32-34, 41, 46). Jesus, who suffered, begged, bled, and died for more passengers, is not any more responsible for those who decided not to board His plane than the airline pilot is responsible for those who decided not to travel on his flight.

Book your flight now (2 Corinthians 6:2) for the friendly-skies flight (1 Thessalonians 4:17) of a lifetime to your eternal vacation spot (Revelation 21:4).

__John 14:6__ Jesus said unto him, "I am the way, the truth, and the life; no man cometh unto the Father, but by Me."

__Matthew 24:30-31__ And then shall appear the sign of the Son of man in heaven; and then shall all the tribes of the earth mourn, and they shall see the Son of man coming in the clouds of heaven with power and great glory. And He shall send His angels with *a great sound of a trumpet, and they shall gather together, His elect from the four winds, from one end of heaven to the other.*

2 Peter 3:9 TLB First, I want to remind you that in the last days there will come scoffers who will do every wrong they can think of, and laugh at the truth.

Romans 10:9 That if you will confess with your mouth the Lord Jesus, and shall believe in your heart that God has raised Him from the dead, you shall be saved.

Matthew 25:34 Then shall the King say to them on His right hand, "Come you blessed of My Father, inherit the kingdom prepared for you from the foundation of the world."

Matthew 25:32-34,41,46 And before him shall be gathered all nations, and He shall separate them one from another, as a shepherd divides his sheep from the goats. And He shall set the sheep on His right hand, and the goats on His left. Then shall the King say to them on His right hand, "Come you blessed of My Father, inherit the kingdom prepared for you from the foundation of the world." Then shall he say also to them on His left hand, "Depart from Me you cursed, into everlasting fire, prepared for the devil and his angels." And these shall go into everlasting punishment, and the righteous into life eternal.

2 Corinthians 6:2 TLB For God says, "Your cry came to Me at a favorable time, when the doors of welcome were wide open. I helped you on a day when salvation was being offered." Behold, now is the accepted time, now is the day of salvation.

1 Thessalonians 4:17 The we which are alive and remain shall be caught up together with them in the clouds, to meet the Lord in the air: and so shall we ever be with the Lord.

Revelation 21:4 And God shall wipe away all tears from their eyes; and there shall be no more death, neither sorrow, nor crying, neither shall there be any more pain; for the former things are passed away.

When evaluating your god, list all the things your god cannot do which will tell you how all-powerfully omnipotent your god is.

Revelation 19:6 And I heard as it were the voice of a great multitude, and as the voice of many waters, and as the voice of mighty thundering, saying, "Alleluia: for the Lord God omnipotent reigns."

Luke 1:37 For with God nothing shall be impossible.

Jeremiah 32:27 Behold, I am the Lord, the God of all flesh: is there anything too hard for Me?

Job 38: 4, 12-13,17-19, 24-25 TLB Where were you when I laid the foundation of the earth? Tell Me, if you know so much. Have you ever commanded the morning to appear and caused the dawn to rise up in the east? Have you ever told the daylight to spread to the ends of the earth, to bring an end to the night's wickedness? Do you know where the gates of death are located? Have you seen the gates of utter gloom? Where is the path to the origin of light? Where is the home of the east wind? Who created a channel for the torrents of rain? Who laid out the path for the lightning?

The Lake of Fire (Revelation 20:15, 9:6, Matthew 7:6) is too good for those swine who walk and trample on the blood and love of Jesus.

Revelation 20:15 And whosoever was not found written in the book of life was cast into the lake of fire.

Revelation 9:6 TLB In those days men shall try to kill themselves but won't be able to – death will not come. They will long to die, but death will flee away.

Matthew 7:6 Give not that which is holy to the dogs, neither cast your pearls before swine, lest they trample them under their feet and turn again and tear you to pieces.

In Genesis Satan was a dangerous serpent (Genesis 3:4-5), but by the end of Revelation he was just a harmless burned worm. (Revelation 20:10).

Genesis 3:4-5 and the serpent said to the woman, "You shall not surely die. For, God knows that your eyes will be opened when you eat it. You will become just like God knowing everything both good and evil."

Revelation 20:10 And the devil that deceived them was cast into the lake of fire and brimstone, where the beast and the false prophet are, and shall be tormented day and night for ever and ever.

Born once, die twice. Born twice, die once.

John 3:3 Jesus answered and said to him, "Verily, verily, I say to you; except a man be born of water and of the Spirit, he cannot enter into the kingdom of God."

John 6:63 TLB Only the Holy Spirit gives eternal life. Those born only once with physical birth will never receive this gift. But, now I have told you how to get this true spiritual life.

God does not grade on the curve allowing the best 70% of mankind to go to heaven.

Romans 3:23 For all have sinned and come short of the glory of God.

John 3:16 For God so loved the world that He gave His only begotten Son that whosoever believes in Him should not perish but have eternal life.

Ephesians 2:8 For by grace are you saved through faith; and that not of yourselves: it is the gift of God.

Matthew 7:14 Because straight is the gate and narrow is the way which leads to life, and few there be that find it.

You are free to decide, but not free not to decide.

John 3:18 He that believes on Him is not condemned, but he that believes not is condemned already, because he has not believed in the name of the only begotten Son of God.

Joshua 24:15 And if it seem evil unto you to serve the Lord, choose you this day whom you will serve ...

Camper awakens in middle of night because she is very hungry. Remembering the apple tree next to her tent, she gets an apple and takes a bite. Something is squirming in her mouth. With a flashlight she sees a worm in the bite. She gets another apple with same result. Still hungry she turns off flashlight and eats wormy apples.

John 3:19-20 And this is the condemnation, that light is come into the world, and men loved darkness rather than light, because their deeds were evil. For everyone that does evil hates the light, neither comes to the light lest his deeds should be exposed.

You can read a cook book just don't try to eat the pages.

__John 5:39-40 TLB__ You search the Scriptures for you believe they give you eternal life. And the Scriptures point to Me. Yet you will not come to Me so that I can give you this life eternal.

A Christian's Life is like making a meal. We find the ingredients in the cookbook recipe which some we like and some we don't. The cookbook has given us the ingredients and directions for a successful meal, but we must provide the effort (2 Timothy 2:15) realizing that the slightest deviation will affect the outcome. We may not see how certain ingredients go together, and why some are essential. For example, we do not like vinegar, but when spices are added to vinegar, we enjoy the dressing on our salad (Matthew 5:44, 47-48).

We prefer the desserts but not the vegetables (James 2:3). We bake a fruit pie without sugar that looks just like one with sugar, but the first bite tells us that it is bitter and not as tasty (Matthew 5:19). A fruit pie with imitation fruit and artificial sweeteners is not a fruit pie but an imitation fruit pie lacking desired qualities (Matthew 24:24).

Soup made with too much water is tasteless and useless (Matthew 25: 2-13). Some ingredients are essential (John 3:7, John 4:24, Acts 4:12, Hebrews 11:6) if what we make can be called a meal. Some entrees are not (Matthew 12:1-2). If we only serve dessert, then this is really not a meal. If we do not serve celery with the main dish, salad, drink, and dessert, we still have a meal.

Likewise, if our main dish is spaghetti and meatballs, but we don't season with oregano, it's still a meal just not as tasty as it could be. If we substitute a cardboard picture of steak even with the proper seasoning, it is tasteless and of no nutritional value.

If our main dish is meat and potatoes, and we serve the meat and potatoes raw, we get our nutrition from this dish, but it is not tasteful leading us eventually to try someone else's cooking.

Guessing at the ingredients and not following all the instructions will lead to disappointment. We may follow all the instructions, however, not putting it in the fire or taking it out of the oven too soon will prove unsuccessful. The right ingredients in the right amount, added at the right time, cooked at the right temperature, and served at the right time as directed by the cookbook provides a successful meal (John 10:10) that will be a joy to eat.

A successful meal served to those who refuse to eat will not benefit those offered (Luke 14:16-18, 23-24). However, when we have eaten a whole meal until full, we are filled with the necessary nutrition to enable us to do our activities (Philippines 1:10-11).

Understand your God-given talents. Don't try preparing sea food if your talent lies in meat and potatoes. God gives us special abilities, use them wisely (1 Corinthians 12:4-5)

__2 Timothy 2:15__ Study to show yourself approved unto God, a workman need not be ashamed, when God examines your work. Know what His word says and means.

__Matthew 5:44, 47-48 TLB__ But, I say, "Love your enemies! Pray for those who persecute you! If you are friendly only to your friends, how are you different from anyone else? Even the heathen do that. But you are to be perfect, even as your Father in heaven is perfect."

__James 2:3 TLB__ And you make a lot of fuss over the rich man and give him the best seat in the house and say to the poor man, "You can stand over there if you like, or else sit on the floor," –well, this kind of action casts a question mark across your faith- are you really a Christian at all? And it shows that you are guided by wrong motives.

Matthew 5:19 **Whosoever, therefore, shall break one of these least commandments, and shall teach men so, he shall be called the least in the kingdom of heaven: but whosoever shall do and teach them, the same shall be called great in the kingdom of heaven.**

Matthew 24:24 **For false Christs shall arise, and false prophets, and will do wonderful miracles, so that if it were possible, even God's chosen ones would be deceived.**

Matthew 25:2-13 TLB *(Note: These verses are not about sharing, but about compromising your Christian principles with worldly non-Biblical principles. You cannot compromise God's truth and still have truth. If you compromise your Biblical beliefs so more people will share the same beliefs, you are not granting more people heaven, but joining those destined for the lake of fire. Watch and pray!)* **But only five of the ten bridesmaids were wise enough to fill their lamps with oil, while the other five were foolish and forgot. So when the bridegroom was delayed they lay down to rest until midnight, when they were roused by the shout, "The bridegroom is coming! Come out and welcome him!" All the girls jumped up and trimmed their lamps. Then the five who hadn't any oil begged the others to share with them, for their lamps were going out. But the others replied, "We haven't enough. Go instead to the shops and buy some for yourselves." But while they were gone, the bridegroom came and those who were ready went in with him to the marriage feast, and the door was locked. Later when the other five returned, they stood outside, calling, "Sir, open the door for us!" But, he called back, "Go away! It is too late." So stay awake and be prepared for you do not know either the day nor the hour wherein the Son of man cometh.**

John 3:7 **Marvel not that I said to you, "You must be born again."**

John 4:24 God is a Spirit: and they that worship Him must worship Him in spirit and truth.

Acts 4:12 Neither is there salvation in any other: for there is none other name under heaven given among men, whereby we must be saved.

Hebrews 11:6 And without faith it is impossible to please Him; for he that comes to God must believe that He is, and that He is a rewarder of them that diligently seek Him.

Matthew 12:1-2 TLB About that time Jesus was walking through some grain fields with His disciples. It was on the Sabbath, the Jewish day of worship, and His disciples were hungry; so they began breaking off heads of wheat and eating the grain. But some Pharisees saw them doing it and protested, "Your disciples are breaking the law. They are harvesting in the Sabbath!"

John 10:10 The thief comes not but for to steal and to kill, and to destroy; I am come that they might have life, and that they might have it more abundantly.

Luke 14:16-18,23-24 TLB Then Jesus replied with this illustration: "A man prepared a great feast and sent out many invitations. When all was ready, he sent his servant around to notify the guests that it was time for them to arrive. But they all began making excuses. 'Well then,' said the master, 'go out into the country lanes and beyond the hedges and urge anyone you find to come so that the house will be full. For none of those I invited first will get even the smallest taste of what I had prepared for them.'"

Philippines 1:10-11 TLB For I want you always to see clearly the difference between right and wrong, and to be inwardly clean, no one being able to criticize you from now until our Lord returns. May you always be doing those good, kind things which show that you are a child of God, for this will bring much praise and glory to the Lord.

1 Corinthians 12: 4-5 Now God gives us many kinds of special abilities, but it is the same Holy Spirit who is the source of them all. There are different kinds of service to God, but it is the same Lord we are serving.

(John 9:6-7) If the man had not washed his eyes as Jesus had commanded, would Jesus have failed? We have no right to blame God until we have heard, read, believed, and followed His instructions. Many still sit and complain that Jesus' instructions are too hard (John 6:60, 66) and blame Him for not bringing the pool to them. (Matthew 10:38)

John 9:6-7 When He had thus spoken, He spit on the ground and made clay of the spit. And anointed the eyes of the blind man with the clay. And said to him, "Go wash in the pool of Siloam (which is by interpretation, Sent)." He went his way, therefore, and washed and came back seeing.

John 6:60,66 Many, therefore, of His disciples when they had heard this, said, "This is very hard to understand. Who can tell what He means?" At this point many of His disciples turned away and deserted Him.

Matthew 10:38 And he that takes not his cross and follows after Me, is not worthy of Me.

Life's storms will not keep you from heaven if you let Jesus into your boat.

John 6:19-21 So when they had rowed about three or four miles out, they see Jesus walking on the sea and drawing near to the ship; and they were afraid. But, He said to them, "It is I, be not afraid. Then they willingly received Him into the ship: and immediately the ship was at the land whither they went.

Love it or leave it are our choices. (John 8:3, 10-12) Because of Christ's forgiveness you can now leave your life of sin or love your life of sin.

John 8:3,5,10-12 And the scribes and Pharisees brought to Him a woman taken in adultery. Now Moses in the law commanded us that such should be stoned; but what do you say? When Jesus had lifted up himself, and saw none but the woman, He said to her, "Woman, where are your accusers? Has no man condemned you? She said, "No man, Lord." And Jesus said to her, "Neither do I condemn you. Go and sin no more."

Accepting the truth is not the problem; "when" is the problem.

Philippians 2:10-11 At the name of Jesus every knee should bow of things in heaven, and things in earth, and things under the earth; and that every tongue should confess that Jesus Christ is Lord, to the glory of God the Father.

2 Corinthians 6:2 TLB For God says, "Your cry came to me at a favorable time, when the doors of welcome were wide open. I helped you on a day when salvation was being offered. Right now God is ready to welcome you. Today, He is ready to save you.

Clint, a civilian EMT student, joined the Army to receive more medical training as a medic. After weeks of classes, studying, and many hours training on cadavers, Clint was assigned to an infantry unit. When Clint's company encountered its first fire fight, wounded soldiers' all around Clint were screaming for a medic.

Like many of us would do, Clint was doing all he could to quickly fill out the forms for a transfer. Clint was a first rate medic when there were no wounded. (John 17:15) God's tests are needed for faith's refinement. Praying for strength and not escape is a sign of Christian maturity. (Matthew 26:42)

__John 17:15__ I pray not that Thou should take them out of the world, but that thou should keep them from evil.

__Matthew 26:42__ He went away again the second time, and prayed, saying, "O My Father, if this cup may not pass away from Me, except I drink it, Thy will be done."

It's half-time and everything that could go wrong has gone wrong. Even your own crowd (Luke 19:36-38) has joined with the opposing team's crowd thunderously booing you (Luke 23:21-23). Your star player is in serious foul trouble and has not been the clutch "go-to" guy many had expected (Matthew 26:74-75). The referees are not being fair as no calls have gone your way (Matthew 27:24-25). Your coach was carried off and pronounced dead (John 19:33-35). Even all your team players are confused, fear for their lives and fled the field. No one has experienced anything like this. Your team was expected to easily win the championship (Mark 11:8-9). Since the game's beginning, the team's confidence has gone from highly confident to zero. *Do you really think you are going to win?* (John 16:33, Revelation 2:7)

__Luke 19:36-38__ And as He went they spread their clothes in the way. And when He was come near, even now at the descent of the mount of Olives, the whole multitude of disciples began to rejoice and praise God with a loud voice for all the mighty works *that they had seen, saying, "Blessed be the King that comes in the name of the Lord: peace in heaven and glory in the highest."*

<u>*Luke 23:21-23*</u> *But they shouted saying, "Crucify Him, Crucify Him." And Pilate said to them a third time, "Why, what evil has He done? I have found no cause of death in Him." I will scourge Him and let Him go." But the voices of the crowd and chief priests prevailed louder that Jesus be crucified.*

<u>*Matthew 26:74-75*</u> *Then, began he to curse and to swear saying, "I never knew the man." And immediately the cock crowed. And Peter remembered the word of Jesus, "Before the cock crows, you shall deny me thrice." And he went out and wept bitterly.*

<u>*Matthew 27:24-25 TLB*</u> *When Pilate saw he wasn't getting anywhere, and that a riot was developing, he sent for a bowl of water and washed his hands before the crowd, saying, "I am innocent of the blood of this good man. The responsibility is yours!" And the mob yelled back, "His blood be on us and on our children!"*

<u>*John 19:33-35*</u> *But when they came to Jesus and saw that He was dead already, they broke not His legs. But one of the soldiers with a spear pierced His side and immediately blood and water came out. And he that saw it bear record, and his record is true: and he knows that he said true that you might believe.*

<u>*Mark 11:8-9*</u> *And many spread their garments in the way: and others cut down branches off the trees and scattered them in the way. And they that went before and they that followed cried, saying, "Hosanna; blessed is He that comes in the name of the Lord."*

John 16:33 *These things have I spoken to you that in me you might have peace. In the world you shall have tribulation, but be of good cheer; I have overcome the world.*

Revelation 2:7 *He that has an ear to hear, let him hear what the Spirit says to the churches. To him that overcomes will I give to eat of the tree of life which is in the midst of the paradise of God.*

No one ever scored a 95-yard touchdown from good field position.

Mark 16:6 *And the angel said to them, "Be not amazed and terrified: you seek Jesus of Nazareth which was crucified: He is risen; He is not here; behold the place where they laid Him.*

For the World Championship Jesus handily defeats the tag team of Sin and Death, (1 Corinthians 15:54-57) yet the latest polls still rank Satan #1 in our lives. *Go figure!*

1 Corinthians 15:54-57 *When this corruptible (perishable part of us) shall have put on incorruption (imperishable), and the mortal (part of us) shall have put on immortality, then shall be brought to pass the saying that is written, Death is swallowed up in victory. O, death where is thy sting? O grave where is thy victory? The sting of death is sin; the strength of sin is the law. But thanks be to God which gives us the victory through our Lord Jesus Christ.*

From Error to Heir: With Jesus no matter how low in the hole you have gone, there is no limit to how high you can fly.

Luke 22:60-62 *And Peter said, "Man I know not what you say." And immediately while he yet spoke, the cock crowed. And the Lord turned and looked upon Peter. And Peter remembered the word of the Lord how He had said to him, "Before the cock crows, you will deny Me three times." And Peter went out and wept bitterly.*

__Matthew 16:18__ And I say also unto you, "That you are Peter, and upon this rock will I build My church; and the gates of hell shall not prevail against it."

__Acts 7:58-60__ And cast Stephen out of the city and stoned him. And the witnesses laid down their clothes at a young man's feet, whose name was Saul. And they stoned Stephen as he called upon God saying, "Lord Jesus, receive my spirit." And he kneeled down, and cried with a loud voice, "Lord, don't charge them with this sin!" And with that he died.

__Acts 8:3__ Saul was like a wild man, going everywhere to devastate the believers, even entering private homes and dragging out men and women alike and jailing them.

__Acts 9:19-20__ Then Saul (Who became Paul) ate and was strengthened. He stayed with the believers in Damascus for a few days. And, went at once to the synagogue to tell everyone there the Good News about Jesus – that He is indeed the Son of God.

God will not judge us by the number or severity of our sins, but by the Light we rejected. (John 3:19-20) Light refused increases darkness. (Romans 1:21)

__John 3:19-20__ And this is the condemnation that Light came into the world, and men loved darkness rather than light, because their deeds were evil. For everyone that does evil hates the Light, neither come to the Light, lest his deeds should be exposed.

__Romans 1:21 TLB__ Yes, they knew about Him all right, but they wouldn't admit or worship Him or even thank Him for all His *daily care. And after awhile they began to think up silly ideas of what God was like and what He wanted them to do. The result was that their foolish minds became dark and confused.*

A friend of mine, the other day, was telling me about leaving church last Sunday. She was feeling extremely blessed with the minister's message, the prayers, and God's presence in her life.

As she walked down the steps rejoicing, another parishioner complained how inappropriate the minister's clothes were, the song selection, and unfriendly church-goers.

The conversation reminded me of the Freedom Flight I took recently. Numerous people donated many hours to say, "Thank you for your service", and provided military veterans with a free flight to Washington D.C. to visit the various national sites.

We boarded busses for the airport at 5:30 am. Motorcyclists lead our caravan and at each overpass were firemen with their fire trucks lighted cheering us on. The airport was filled with well-wishers thanking us for our service. The flight attendants were gracious as they served us meals.

At Washington D. C. lines of well-wishers were formed for us to walk through as they thanked us for our service. The awesome tour went well as we saw war memorials to those who served, and historic federal buildings.

Late afternoon we returned to the airport for our flight home. On the return flight we had mail call. Hometown high school students had written us letters thanking us for our service. We read the letters as we ate the fourth meal served to us that day.

As a Vietnam veteran I remembered that it was 16 years after my tour in Vietnam before anyone, besides another soldier, said, "Thanks." I leaned back in my seat reminiscing about all the people that awoke early and stayed late just to thank us. As I relished in the closure of a 45-year old hurt, the freedom flight attendee seated next to me complained about the quality of food and the length of the day.

As I quietly listened to his complaints, I remembered a scripture (Matthew 7:7) "Seek and ye shall find." If you seek to complain about the minister, the church service, or the work that thankful, loving people planned, you will find. Conversely, if you seek to find God in those things, you will find.

There is a loving God who gave us a garden to live in where He would walk with us. When mankind trashed the Garden with sin, God sent His innocent Son to teach us and to die painfully (Matthew 27:50) for our sins giving us the opportunity to dine with Him in paradise. Because of His unending love, He will return again to reward those who love Him with a heavenly home.

Many (Matthew 27:42) condemn Jesus for not having the power to come down off the cross while others rejoice that He had the power to stay on the cross. Seek and ye shall find. Many curse, deny, and hate God; while others who seek Him, find His love, forgiveness, and grace. What are you seeking? What will you find?

Matthew 7:7 *Ask and it shall be given you, seek and you shall find; knock and it shall be opened unto you.*

Matthew 27:50 *Jesus, when He had cried again with a loud voice, yielded up the Ghost.*

THE AUTHOR

***Matthew 27:42** He saved others; himself He cannot save. If He be the King of Israel, let Him now come down from the cross, and we will believe Him.*

(Disclaimer: I know nothing about Mr. Steinbrenner, his faith, or his inheritance. This parable was revealed to me as I read of his death. This is a parable that uses Mr. Steinbrenner's name and is only a parable nothing more.)

I'm really excited about being named in George Steinbrenner's (New York Yankee's owner) will. I really didn't ever meet or personally know George, but I liked some of his qualities. He paid well, was generous at times, and was a self-made billionaire.

I'm really not a Yankee fan, but I liked George. I knew he wasn't just some fictitious <u>Seinfeld</u> character, but really existed. He demanded loyalty, and I never remember saying anything against him, although I didn't always like his decisions. I was frustrated that his Yankees won so much since I am a White Sox fan, but I believe George was a good person, and I always cheered for his team against the National League.

This summer I was saddened to hear George died. However, if I'm to get my inheritance, I guess he had to die. I intend to share my inheritance with my church. I'm going to send them a postcard from Hawaii!

So, because I liked George, never really said anything bad about him, thought he was a good man, and even cheered for his team occasionally, I am confident I will be named in his will.

Are you going to heaven? Jesus said, "I am the way. No one comes to the Father, but by me." (John 14:16) Some think there are other ways to heaven such as good deeds, good parents, church attendance, never saying anything bad about Jesus, saying Jesus was a good person, etc. Is your reasoning to get to heaven the same as my reasoning to be named in Mr. Steinbrenner's will?

If George Steinbrenner were alive today, and I asked him for my inheritance what do you think he would say? (Matthew 7:22-23) If you don't think I will inherit the New York Yankee fortune, then why do you believe when you die, you will go to heaven? Satan, the great deceiver, (Revelations 12:9) has convinced us that God is a mean-spirited bully who likes to punish us, when the opposite is true. God loves us. That is a fact. The question is do you want God's love.

Think about it. Would God send His Son to die a torturous death if there was another way? (Luke 22:42) It is *your* responsibility to find the way to eternal joy with someone that loved you so much He (Romans 6:23) paid the ultimate price for your admission.

__John 14:6__ Jesus said unto him, "I am the way, the truth, and the life; no man cometh unto the Father, but by Me."

__Matthew 7:22-23__ Not everyone that says unto me, "Lord, Lord, shall enter into the kingdom of heaven; but he that does the will of My Father which is in heaven. Many will say to Me in that day, 'Lord, Lord, have we not prophesied in Your name; and in Your name cast out devils; and in Your name done many wonderful works?'" And then I will profess to them, "I never knew you; depart from Me you that do iniquity.

__Revelation 12:9__ And the great dragon was cast out, that old serpent, called the devil, and Satan which deceives the whole world: he was cast out into the earth, and his angels were cast out with him.

Luke 22:42 Saying, "Father, if thou be willing, remove this cup from Me: nevertheless not My will, but, thine be done."

Romans 6:23 For the wages of sin is death; but the gift of God is eternal life through Jesus Christ our Lord.

Good deeds are one of the greatest stumbling blocks to heaven.

Isaiah 64:6 But we all are as an unclean thing, and all our righteousness are as filthy rags; and we all do fade as a leaf; and our iniquities like the wind have taken us away.

Ephesians 2:8-9 For by grace (unmerited favor) are you saved through faith; and that not of yourselves: it is a gift of God. Not of works lest any man should boast.

Matthew 7:22-23 Many will say to me in that day, "Lord, Lord have we not prophesied in thy name; and in thy name have cast out devils; and in thy name done many wonderful works?" and then I will profess to them, "I never knew you: depart from Me you that work iniquity."

There is a lot of forgiveness that doesn't get used.

John 3:16 For God so loved the world that He gave His only begotten Son that, whosoever believes on him shall not perish but have eternal life.

Romans 10:9-10 TLB If you tell others with your own mouth that Jesus Christ is your Lord, and believe with your own heart that God raised Him from the dead, you will be saved. For it is by believing in his heart that a man becomes right with God; and with his mouth he tells others of his faith, confirming his salvation.

Matthew 23:37 O Jerusalem, Jerusalem, thou that killest the prophets, and stonest them which are sent unto thee how often would I have gathered thy children together, even as a hen gathers her chickens under her wings, and ye would not.

In church many sing, "Just As I Am," and leave just as they were.

1 Corinthians 1:18 For the preaching of the cross is to them that perish foolishness; but to us which are saved, it is the power of God.

"Savior" is to "Lord" what "Love" is to "Need." Everyone loves a Savior with His physical miracles when they really need a Lord with His eternal-life teachings (John 6: 26). If you only ask for the Savior's miracles, you will not get a Savior, but if you ask for a Lord to lead your life, you'll get a Savior and a Lord (John 6:68). Satan will perform physical miracles, but he cannot give you spiritual eternal life (Matthew 24:24).

Miraculous physical healings to a terminal, decaying body are certainly interest grabbing and wonderful. However, they are pale in comparison with the spiritual miracle of a sin-infested soul becoming worthy of a holy, heavenly eternal life (John 3:16). Lazarus was physically raised from the dead (John 11:43-44), but where is his physical body now? Thomas finally realized what he needed (John 20:27-28).

The world wants a Savior to heal and return them to their sinful ways. Few (Matthew 7:14) want a life-style changing Lord to guide them toward an earthly abundant life and a heavenly paradise (Revelation 21:4).

John 6:26 Jesus replied, "The truth of the matter is that you want to be with Me because I fed you, not because you believe in Me.

John6:68 Then, Simon Peter answered Him, "Lord, to whom shall we go? You have the words of eternal life.

Matthew 24:24 For there shall arise false Christs, and false prophets, and shall show great signs and wonders; insomuch that, if it were possible, they shall deceive God's chosen ones.

John 3:16 For God so loved the world that He gave His only begotten Son that whosoever believes on Him shall have everlasting life.

John 11:43-44 And when He thus had spoken, He cried with a loud voice, "Lazarus, come forth!' And he that was dead came forth, bound hand and foot with grave clothes: and his face was bound about with a napkin. Jesus said to them, "Loose him and let him go."

John 20:27-28 Then Jesus said to Thomas, "Reach out your finger here and see My hands: and put your hand and place it in My side. Do not be faithless, but believing." And Thomas answered and said to Him, "My Lord and my God."

Matthew 7:14 Because straight is the gate and narrow is the way which leads to eternal life, and few there be that find it.

Revelation 21:4 And God shall wipe away all tears from their eyes, and there shall be no more death, neither sorrow, nor crying, neither shall there be any more pain: for the former things shall be passed away.

The owner of the company for which I work fired Stan, an employee with considerable tenure, for theft, insubordination, and actions detrimental to the company. (Luke 10:18) Stan wanted to take over the company in a power move that would have eliminated the owner and only benefitted Stan.

Since that day Stan has tried his best for revenge on his former boss. To put it mildly Stan hates him and has said many untruthful things about his former boss.

Much to everyone's surprise our boss's daughter started dating Stan. No one can figure this out. Doesn't she know about Stan? Is she doing this to hurt her father who has been wonderful to her? Is she just naïve?

Stan is a great salesman and charmer (2 Corinthians 11:14), no doubt about that, who always seems to say the right words to get his results. (Revelation 12:9) He is older and wiser than the boss's daughter and somehow she believes everything he says. Stan is cunning, and she is outmatched.

Because of all our dealings with Stan, my fellow employees and I know Stan's motives. (1 Peter 5:8) He doesn't love her he just hates her dad and wants to take the possession our boss loves the most.

I can list many acts of love her dad has done for her because he loves her (1 Peter 2:24). On the other hand, Stan has done nothing for the boss's daughter's welfare that wasn't for his own benefit. Her dad's love should speak louder than Stan's hollow lies. I guess her hearing is impaired (Matthew 13:43). She must realize who really loves her (John 3:16). If she knew where he lives and what lifestyle (Galatians 5:19-21) she is giving up to be with this deceiver, she better hope it's not too late for her dad to take her back if she comes to her senses.

The latest is Stan has proposed marriage to her and has promised her the world. Her dad has done everything in his power to persuade her to refuse Stan's glamorous lies (Galatians 5:18). Why she doesn't believe her dad who has never lied to her and accepts Stan's temporary fun is a mystery. Immediate pleasure (Hebrews 11:25) often trumps eternal, clear-to-the-bone joy (Galatians 5:22-23).

Satan doesn't love us; he hates God. Because we are God's most prized possession (John 3:16, 1John 4:16, 19, 1 Thessalonians 5:10), Satan tries to destroy us (Revelation 20:15). He has no feelings for us just hatred for the One who really loves us. Pleasure vs. Love?

<u>Luke 10:18</u> And He said to them, "I beheld Satan as lightning fall from heaven."

<u>2 Corinthians 11:14</u> Yet I am not surprised! Satan can change himself (masquerades) into an angel of light.

<u>1 Peter 5:8</u> Be sober, be vigilant, because your adversary the devil, as a roaring lion, walks about seeking whom he may devour.

<u>1 Peter 2:24</u> Who His own self bore our sins in His own body on the tree, that we, being dead to sins, should live unto righteousness: by whose stripes you are healed.

<u>Matthew 13:43</u> Then shall the righteous shine forth as the sun in the kingdom of their Father. Who has ears to hear, let him hear.

<u>John 3: 16</u> For God so loved the world that He gave His only begotten Son that whosoever believes on Him shall not perish but have everlasting life.

<u>Galatians 5:19-21</u> But when you follow your own wrong inclinations your lives will produce these evil results: impure thoughts, eagerness for lustful pleasure, idolatry, witchcraft (encouraging the activity of demons), hatred and fighting,

jealousy and anger, constant effort to get the best for yourself,
complaints and criticisms, the feeling that everyone else is wrong
except those in your own little group – and there will be wrong
doctrine, envy, murder, drunkenness, wild parties, and all that
sort of thing. Let me tell you again as I have before that anyone
living that sort of life will not inherit the kingdom of God.

Galatians 5:18 But if you are lead by the spirit, you are not
under the law.

Hebrews 11:25 Choosing rather to suffer affliction with the
people of God, than to enjoy the pleasures of sin for a season.

Galatians 5:22-23 But the fruit of the Spirit is love, joy, peace,
longsuffering, gentleness, goodness, faithfulness, meekness, self-
control: against such there is no law.

1 John 4:16,19 And we have known and believed the love that
God has for us. God is love; and he that dwells in love dwells in
God, and God in him.

1 Thessalonians 5:10 TLB He died for us so that we can live
with Him forever, whether we are dead or alive at the time of
His return.

Revelation 20:15 And whosoever was not found written in the
book of life was cast into the lake of fire.

If you keep on doing what you've always done, you'll keep on getting
what you've always got.

Acts 26:1, 13-18 TLB Then King Agrippa said to Paul, "Go
ahead, tell us your story." So Paul, with many gestures, presented
his defense. When one day about noon, sir, a light from heaven

*brighter than the sun shone down on me and my companions;
We all fell down, and I heard a voice speaking to me in Hebrew,
'Saul, Saul, why are persecuting Me? You are only hurting
yourself.' "Who are you, sir?" I asked. And the Lord replied, "I
am Jesus, the one you are persecuting. Now stand up. For I have
appeared to you to appoint you as My servant and witness. You
are to tell the world about this experience and about the many
other occasions when I shall appear to you. And I will protect you
from your own people and the Gentiles. Yes, I am going to send
you to the Gentiles to open their eyes to their true condition so
that they may repent and live in the light of God instead of in
Satan's darkness, so that they may receive forgiveness for their
sins, and God's inheritance along with all everywhere whose sins
are cleansed away, who are set apart by faith in Me.*

For what did you sell your birthright? (Genesis 25:33-34, 1 John 3:1)

*Genesis 25:32-34 And Jacob said, "Look, I am dying of
starvation!" said Essau. "What good is my birthright?" "Swear
to me this day, and he swore to him: and he sold his birthright
to Jacob. Then Jacob gave Essau some bread and lentil stew.
Essau ate and drank and rose up and went about his business,
indifferent to the fact that he had sold his birthright.*

*Matthew 26:14-15 Then Judas Iscariot, one of the twelve apostles,
went to the chief priests, and asked, "How much will you pay me
to get Jesus into your hands?" And they gave him thirty pieces of
silver.*

*John 12:43 For they loved the praise of men more than the praise
of God.*

1 John 3:1 Behold, what manner of love the Father has bestowed upon us, that we should be called the sons of God: therefore, the world knows us not because it knew Him not.

The question everyone must answer, (Mark 8:27-29) "Who is Jesus?" Is He your despised servant/Savior who will not do what you command of Him? (1 Peter3:12) Or, is He your Lord/God whom you allow to lovingly guide and protect you in the paths of righteousness? (Psalms 23:3-4)

Mark 8:11 When the local Jewish leaders learned of His arrival, they came to argue with Him. "Do a miracle for us," they said, "Make something happen in the sky. Then we will believe in you."

Mark 8:27-29 And Jesus went out and His disciples, into the towns of Caesarea Philippi: and by the way He asked His disciples, saying to them, "Whom do men say that I am?" And they answered, "John the Baptist: but some say, Elias; and others, One of the prophets." And He said to them, "But whom say you that I am?" And Peter answered and said to Him, "Thou are the Christ."

1 Peter 3:12 For the eyes of the Lord are over the righteous, and his ears are open to their prayers: But the face of the Lord is against them that do evil.

Psalms 23:3-4 He restores my soul: He leads me in the paths of righteousness for His name's sake. Yea, though I walk through the valley of the shadow of death, I will fear no evil; for thou art with me, Thy rod and Thy staff they comfort me.

The first coming of Jesus was to rescue the lost sinners (John 3:17); His second coming will be to reward us. (Hebrews 9:28) What will be your reward? (Revelation 20: 12, 15)

John 3:17 *For God sent not His Son into the world to condemn the world, but that the world through Him might be saved.*

Hebrews 9:28 *So Christ died only once as an offering for the sins of many people; and He will come again, but not to deal again with our sins. This time He will come bringing salvation to all those who are eagerly and patiently waiting for Him.*

Revelation 20:12,15 TLB *I saw the dead, great and small, standing before God; and The Books were opened, including the Book of Life. And the dead were judged according to the things written in The Books, each according to his deeds. And if anyone's name was not found recorded in the Book of Life, he was thrown into the Lake of Fire.*

The *show must go on!* Since Jesus has ascended into heaven, we must *show* the tumultuous world the love of God. We must *show* the miracle of acceptance when tragedy hits. We must *show* victory in trials, *show* compassion; *show* benefits of serving a risen Savior; *show* peace in storms; *show* the spiritually blind how to see; *show* others how to boldly and faithfully pray, "Thy will be done." *The show must go on!* (Mark 16:15)

Mark 16:15 *And He said to them, "Go into all the world and preach the gospel to every creature.*

He who hath ears to hear, let him hear. (Matthew 13:43)

Matthew 13:43 *Then shall the righteous shine forth as the sun in the kingdom of their Father. Who has ears to hear, let him hear.*

AMEN

EPILOGUE

If God has spoken to you through this unique Bible study; if you want to start on the road to an earthly abundant life and an eternal heavenly home with a God who has proven again and again His love for you. If you want Him to come into your life, then you must ask for His help. Since God does not force himself on you, you must ask, and God will do the rest guiding you on that narrow path to glory.

<u>Pray</u>: *Dear Lord, I am a sinner who wants forgiveness. Please come into my heart. I believe you are the one true God and Jesus, who, willingly shed His blood to cover my sins, is my Savior. Please make your presence in me felt and lead me in the paths of righteousness. Thank you for delivering me from the eternal screams and gnashing of teeth in the Lake of Fire* (Matthew 13:41-42) *to eternally dining with you in a no-death, no-sorrow, no-tears, no-pain heaven.* (Revelation 21:4)

Since you have now declared your life's "major", you need to find trusted instructors who will teach and assist you. <u>Pray</u> for a Bible church. <u>Pray</u> for instructors of God's word. <u>Pray</u> for Christian friends to help. Pray God will help you find the right ones. <u>Pray</u>. <u>Pray</u> for strength, <u>pray</u> praise, <u>pray</u> for needs, <u>pray</u> for inner peace, always end your <u>prayers</u> with, "Thy will be done." Oh, yes, and did I mention to <u>PRAY</u>!?

God has no <u>prayer</u> quota. You can <u>pray</u> as many times as you want, whenever you want, with whatever is on your mind. There is no formal way of <u>praying</u>. Remember, your loving God is always excited to hear from you. Revelation 5:8 says your <u>prayers</u> are as *sweet incense* to God.

Congratulations! I can hardly wait to someday meet you in heaven!

In His love,
The Author

P.S. Don't be afraid to reread this book. Rereading is usually as beneficial as the first reading. Please share this book with someone you love who may be difficult to talk to about your faith.